PERPETUAL MOTION

*To Chris, all my achievements are our achievements.
And to the people: we are all champions at something.*

PERPETUAL MOTION

RAY PRICE
WITH NEIL CADIGAN

ANGUS & ROBERTSON PUBLISHERS

Angus & Robertson Publishers
Unit 4, Eden Park, 31 Waterloo Road
North Ryde, NSW, Australia 2113, and
16 Golden Square, London WIR 4BN
United Kingdom.

© Ray Price 1987

Designed and produced by
John Ferguson Pty Ltd
100 Kippax St
SURRY HILLS 2010

This book is copyright. Apart from any fair dealing for the purposes of private study, research, criticism or review, as permitted under the Copyright Act, no part may be reproduced by any process without written permission. Inquiries should be addressed to the publisher.

First published in Australia
by Angus & Robertson Publishers in 1987

National Library of Australia
Cataloguing-in-publication entry

   Price, Ray.
      Perpetual motion.

   ISBN 0 207 15694 8.

   1. Price, Ray. 2. Rugby football players – Australia – Biography. I. Title.

796.33′3′0924

Typeset in 11/13 pt Times by G.T. Setters Pty Limited
Printed in Australia by
Australian Print Group, Maryborough, Vic.

Contents

Acknowledgements	vi
Foreword	vii
The Highest Note	1
Valley Boy	8
Union Days	19
On the Wallaby Tour	33
The Switch	42
Rugby League—The Beginning	48
September Sadness	56
The Hartley Feud	65
The 14th Kangaroos	76
The Invincibles	86
Coach John Peard	95
Jack Gibson and Success	105
From Big Jack to Little John	118
War Games	128
Farewell Australia	136
The Crow and I	144
The Price to Pay	154
My Canterbury Hate	166
The Sometimes Philosopher	174
A Look Back	187

Acknowledgements

I WOULD DEARLY like to thank the many people who helped this autobiography come to fruition: Those who helped jog my memory and who helped Neil Cadigan (Caddo) check on dates and events, particularly his *Rugby League Week* colleagues Norm Tasker (my old mate) and David Middleton, and my wife Chris who sat with me and acted as my interviewer through endless hours of taping my recollections and opinions for Caddo to put onto paper.

This book was the brainchild of John White, and as throughout my whole career, his guidance and assistance has been priceless.

But my biggest thankyou goes to Caddo, who put in many late nights and many more hours than I did in making this book what it is. He picked my brains, he encouraged me and made this book a real team effort.

My thanks also go to Tony Love, from John Ferguson Pty Ltd, publishers, who did a great job of editing and to John Anderson who has shown great enthusiasm in wanting to make the book a publishing success.

Some of the photographs were used from my own collection, and I owe many thanks to photographers from the News Ltd and Fairfax organisations for supplying me with them over the years. Other photos came from the files of *Rugby League Week*.

Foreword

WHO CAN FORGET the drama and emotion of that day in 1986 when Ray Price announced his retirement. He had captained Parramatta to a thrilling grand final win over Canterbury-Bankstown. That day saw the retirement of two of those great players. As Ray says, he wanted to end with Michael Cronin, the greatest footballer he ever stood beside. And what a fitting venue for such a farewell; the Sydney Cricket Ground, with its golden memories of so many other great contests featuring the greatest rugby players the world has seen.

That day also said a great deal about Ray Price, the man. He said after that game that he wanted to be remembered as a winner and that is how he will be remembered. There could hardly be any doubt about his toughness. Even in the toughest league Ray stood out. How many times have we seen Ray drag himself to his feet when other players would have retired gracefully to the grandstand. His last game was also a testimony to his courage, his absolute commitment, and to his love for the game to which he had dedicated so many years.

To be a star, it is said, takes five per cent talent and 95 per cent dedication. Ray had more talent than that, and more dedication. He was a real star, the best in the game. A dual international, Ray represented Australia at Rugby Union before turning to League. But he was, first and foremost, a Parramatta man. He grew up in the area and he played all his senior football, League and Union, with Parramatta. Perhaps I am permitted to demonstrate some bias by remarking that this, of course, reflects his excellent judgement. His great loyalty to the club and particularly his feeling of camaraderie and his support of his team-mates, shines through his story.

And what a marvellous story it is, presented in Ray Price's own direct way. It is a story of great warmth, yet some anger, and fun and excitement, told by a quintessential Australian.

I am particularly thrilled that Ray acknowledges my part in getting Parramatta its magnificent stadium, in my view the best club ground in the world. That is one of my proudest achievements. And some of my happiest memories are of having seen Ray play there with the Eels.

For Chris, his wife, and his children Ben and Kasey I have enormous admiration. It is not easy to live with someone as committed to his calling as was Ray Price, but, they supported him constantly.

This book is, in my view, a celebration of the virtues which have made Australia the great country, of which all Australians should be justly proud. Hard working, tough, courageous, talented, warm, humorous and unpretentious. Those are the qualities I admire in Australians and Ray Price, Mr Perpetual Motion, demonstrated them all in abundance during his long career.

On behalf of all those thousands who thrilled to your performances across the world Ray, I say thanks for the memories! We can all relive them through the publication of this, the Ray Price story.

The Hon. John Brown M.P.
Minister for the Arts, Sport, The Environment, Tourism and Territories.

The Highest Note

I WAS SCARED. What I was about to do was going to be the toughest thing I had faced in my life. I was supposed to be so happy, having just won the ultimate Rugby League goal, a premiership, but I felt so sad, knowing that I was about to make one final announcement.

I had rehearsed what I was going to say time and time again in my mind, that this would be the end, but I put it out of my mind during the game. Once the full-time hooter went and Parramatta had won the 1986 title by 4–2 in the first-ever tryless grand final, I looked for my footballing mate Mick Cronin. I put my arm around him and said, "We've done it Crow. We can go out on the highest note." That meant as much to me as anything else; that Crow was able to come back from a shocking eye injury early in the 1986 season and finish with me.

But when I had to get up on that dais in front of the Prime Minister of Australia, Bob Hawke, and cough up those few words to the huge gathering of football fans there at the Sydney Cricket Ground, a wave of terror went through me.

"This is the proudest moment of my career. And it's the last time I play here." They were only a few words, but I choked and staggered on them. They were like a baby's first words, so hard to get out. I scraped through and walked away from the microphone. I couldn't say anything else. A dream had just been realised.

Retiring is a frightening thing for anyone in professional sport. It is not just giving up a sport or a hobby. It means changing your entire life, because Rugby League at the highest level completely dominates your life and that of your family.

The beauty of giving it all away is the timing. I could not have been luckier. I didn't want the white boots episode that still haunts

Graeme Langlands. I didn't want to be a John Raper or a Billy Smith or a Tom Raudonikis. I wanted to end at the top.

I quickly looked around at the sea of faces at the SCG, shook hands with I don't know who, stepped down from the dais, picked up the Giltinan Shield and found Mick Cronin's shoulder. There was a victory lap to be made. And a goodbye to the SCG Hill.

The Crow and I were in no hurry to get around that famous oval because we knew it was our last lap of the SCG as players. As we skirted the picket-fence we acknowledged the fans, shook more hands, signed more autographs. We made sure we stopped for a good while in front of the Hill, in front of my type of people.

Then out of the blue someone passed each of us a can of Tooheys. I was shocked really, not so much at myself because I knew I'd drink it, but the Crow? He was a Bacardi man; he never touched the beer. But there we were strolling around the SCG, sipping on a Tooheys each. Our mouths were so dry and the cans were ice-cold. Chilled like my spine.

I felt sad more than elated. And drained. That's why we took so long to get around. The other players kept stopping and waiting for us to catch up because we had lagged so far behind. But this day meant more to me than any other in my career. More than anything else I'd achieved. I had attained my one final and greatest goal: to captain Parramatta to a premiership. I had gone out on top.

Later that afternoon Crow and I were standing out in the middle of the SCG in pitch darkness posing for photographs. It was our testimonial year and while all the other players were in the dressing-room popping corks, I didn't mind being out in the middle one more time for the media, who had done everything they could to make it a memorable year. When they asked us to go back out onto the oval it was really very touching.

It was an eerie feeling. Everything was dark except for the old members stand. I looked around at the other stands and the memories started flooding back, just racing through my mind. So many great things had happened to me at the ground, and many bad.

I played my first Test, in Rugby Union, and scored a try in the left-hand corner in front of the Hill, right in front of my family and friends. I pictured myself playing my first Rugby League grand final, in 1976 against Manly. I always thought we were going to win that game right up to the very end. Then there was the grand-final

The Highest Note

replay in 1977 when I got used as a punching bag by Rod Reddy, who knew he wasn't going to stay on the paddock and had been sent out to put me out of the game. And that first Parramatta premiership in 1981, when the Bear, Bob O'Reilly, just about cried. So nearly did I.

Little things like scoring certain tries, certain Tests, the whole State of Origin thing, all flashed before me. It was almost scary on the one hand, fantastic on the other.

When I got back to the dressing room, it was a bit disappointing. People were saying that Canterbury thought they were unlucky to have lost and that we had been dead lucky. A few more minutes and we couldn't have held on. It really dampened the victory. Canterbury couldn't accept losing to a side they always thought they would beat. We fought hard for that game and had finished the season beating Canterbury the last three times we'd met. As far as I was concerned we had come up with the big-time games when it counted. We should have won that grand final by 10 to 15 points; we had two dead-set tries disallowed, and if they had been awarded to us we would have run away with it.

But after all had been said and done, we had the Winfield Cup, so we got stuck into the celebrating. The fact that Michael Cronin and I were retiring, however, overtook feelings a bit. The players wanted to see us go out on a winning note. I think it meant more to them than it did to us, and that was a whole lot. Players like Peter Sterling, Brett Kenny, Steve Ella and Eric Grothe, whom we had played with for six or seven years, wanted that victory more for us than themselves. That was Parramatta. They'd bleed before they'd stop. They gave us everything.

The next thing, I found myself sitting down on some old wooden steps with Bob Hawke. He was recalling the last time he had been in our dressing room, three years earlier, when we had last won the competition. He was going for the big trifecta then. He'd tipped Hawthorn in the Aussie Rules on the Saturday, Parramatta in the League on the Sunday, and had his money on Australia winning the America's Cup the next week. And they did. He got the big three.

In 1986 he was hoping for the same trifecta. Again Hawthorn had won the Rules on the Saturday, we took the honours again on the Sunday, and he was waiting only for victory in the America's Cup in January.

He asked me if I was going over to Perth for the America's Cup.

Perpetual Motion

I was saying, "No", when the Crow came over and sat next to me.

"Well how would you like to go over and see the Cup," said the Prime Minister.

"Bob, of course we would like to take our wives to see the Cup. It would be great. If you want to invite us, we'd love to go," I said cheekily. (You can't take the fibro out of this boy!)

Mr Hawke turned to his secretary and said, "Make sure you ring these people and arrange their travel and accommodation and have them over to witness the America's Cup."

And the guy did. We ended up in Perth in January, guests of the Prime Minister, to see the Cup. It was an absolutely fantastic time, too, except for one thing: because *Stars and Stripes* had given our *Kookaburra* boys such a flogging in the final series, we arrived the day after the last race instead of right in the middle of the big climax as planned. It didn't stop us enjoying ourselves though.

I had always admired Bob Hawke and it was a pretty special moment being able to sit in a crowded room, mayhem all around us, and have a man-to-man chat, Mr Hawke sipping his orange juice, me with a beer. That's another thing I admired about him. He was able to give up drinking and stick at it no matter what the occasion. That day there were plenty of the Parramatta players, cocky after a grand final victory, geeing him up with "Have some champers, Bob, c'mon have a drink with us Bob". He politely stuck to the juice.

He didn't stay long in the room, but while he was there he was most welcome. It's good to have a Prime Minister genuinely interested in sport, and I think we had turned him into a genuine Parramatta supporter as well. He obviously admired the way we played and he could see our team spirit first hand.

After he left the back-slappers flooded in, congratulating the Crow and I on the victory and our careers. It had happened on this day of the year before, but there was something special about 1986. It was all sincerity.

Then came along one man who'd been like a godfather to me, a man who had adopted me in many ways and had taken upon himself to look after my business affairs. Most people call John White my manager. I remember just grabbing yet another hand that was pointed my way and giving it a shake. I can't remember what Whitey said to me at first, but it made me look up and see the incredible smile of satisfaction he had. John White was another person who knew how important it was that I finished a

My last moments as a player on the victory dias at the Sydney Cricket Ground. It meant so much to me that Mick Cronin was able to share his moments as a player with me and the greatest prizes Sydney can offer, the Winfield Cup and the J.J. Giltinan Shield.

winner. I knew how much he had been willing me on, and for a second I looked at him and thought how much I owed him and how special it was that I could make him feel just as tall as I felt right then and there.

I don't know how long we stayed in that old, dingy dressing room at the SCG, the inner sanctum for players after a grand final. I think the bus left at about 7.30 pm, nearly three hours after the full-time hooter had gone. The other guys all fought through the cheering mob at the members bar, saw their wives and girl friends, and hopped onto the bus back to Parramatta Leagues Club.

I'd always been allowed to make my own way to the SCG; it was a kind of idiosyncrasy. I'd drive in with my wife Chris, park the car and meet the bus in Moore Park, then travel into the oval with them. On the way back to the club, we'd do things in reverse.

I went home and saw the kids, like I had always done, dropped my gear off, dropped the car off in Parramatta, and got the bus to pick me up on the way to the club. When we got there, it was absolute chaos. But it was fantastic.

They had a table-top truck outside the front of the club and the idea was for us to hop off the bus and onto the truck to be introduced to the thousands of people who couldn't get inside the club, which by this stage was bursting at the seams.

There were people about 60 or 70 deep around this truck. The bus pulled up beside it and off we piled, and it was as if the crowd were lifting us onto the truck. We were virtually walking on their shoulders. It was one of the most amazing scenes I've ever witnessed.

One by one we were introduced to the crowd. The noise was deafening. All these people had just come to say "Well done", and give us the heroes' welcome they thought we deserved. I thought of the first time I had gone back to the club, in 1976 after we had lost to Manly. We were so dejected after going down that day, but when we got back to the club it was packed, everyone was cheering and telling us how proud they were that we had gone so close. It was the same every time we went back after a grand final, win or lose. That's why you can never forget the fans; without them we wouldn't have the game of Rugby League. And you can never forget how special they can make you feel. I was a boy from the rough-and-tough western Sydney suburb of Dundas. I was just like them, but they had lifted me to a special position in their lives. That's what is so great about sport.

The Highest Note

We were hustled straight into the club and to the auditorium. I reckon there were 10 times more people in the auditorium than it was supposed to hold. It was so hot and sweaty. People were fainting, some had cuts, some were standing on tables and on other people's shoulders. It must have been so uncomfortable for them, but they just wanted to see the players and give us all a big welcome home.

They were singing the old familiar chant. Parra (stomp, stomp, stomp) ... Parra (stomp, stomp, stomp). The whole floor of the auditorium was vibrating. All the players were on the stage and one by one they were asked to speak. The people loved it and so did we.

I'll never forget that night, probably because I knew I wouldn't be going through anything like that again. I took it in more than I had done in the past. It felt great that I could give something back to the Parra fans who had supported the team right through my 11 years there. I can't speak highly enough of Parramatta people. If every other club had supporters like the Eels, Rugby League would be in a much healthier situation.

The night went on and on, as did the celebrations. I called it quits about 1 am, and was probably the first player to hit the sack.

The next day was like most Mondays after a grand final. Our ritual was to go to Brian Hambly's Albion Hotel at Parramatta. Everyone just called it Grumpy's Pub. All the other guys kept geeing me up, telling me I wouldn't retire, that I'd back-up the next year. They'd all more or less expected I was finishing, but I wouldn't admit a thing; I had planned all along that I wouldn't announce my intentions until after the grand final. I wanted to keep people guessing and I wanted the satisfaction of holding up the Winfield Cup and making the announcement to everyone at once.

I had told my wife Chris that win, lose or draw, it was the end. I don't think she felt so sure. If I'd lost, maybe I might have backed-up, even though I'd promised myself I wouldn't. I could have gone another season, but not at the pace I was used to. I would have struggled, at the age of 34, to live up to my own standards, and that wasn't the way I was going to go out. Winning the grand final on my last day might make it easy to say in hindsight, but the time was right. It was perfect.

Valley Boy

BELIEVE IT OR not, I was born in silvertail country, slap bang in the middle of Sydney's North Shore. It was the fourth of March, 1953. My mother has often told me the story of a student doctor at the Royal North Shore Hospital in St Leonards, who picked up all 4.3 kilograms (9lb 9oz) of me not long after I was born at 5.30 p.m. and, with a touch of ESP, declared, "He'll play for Australia—in the front row!"

Years later, when I first turned to Rugby League, my Parramatta coach Terry Fearnley reckoned I could play lock, second-row, or hooker. Second-row was bad enough, and one of the greatest accomplishments of my career was never having played hooker, but that medico's forecast of the front-row—no way. I'm glad that young doctor, whoever he was, was right with only the first half of his prediction.

I can only vaguely remember my days in "toff" territory. I lived there during my first four years, with my mother's parents at Neutral Bay; in Watson Street, just down the road from a supermarket called the Big Bear.

My grandfather sometimes took us down to North Sydney Oval No. 2 to play cricket or just muck around on the swings and slippery dip. Grandad George Thomas was a pretty good Rugby Union player who apparently went close to Australian selection when a broken leg did him in. He played for Northern Suburbs and later turned to League, playing with Norths and Balmain.

My father's parents lived at Milsons Point and were reasonably well off; wealthy enough to send Dad to boarding school at St Josephs at Hunters Hill. I don't think he was really keen on the idea and quite often, the story goes, it would be a dead heat who arrived first back at the Milsons Point home after his parents had

Valley Boy

dropped him off at the start of term. That's one thing, other than football, that I shared with my father; our "love" of school.

My silvertail connection goes further. International League lock Peter Diversi married my mother's sister Dawn in 1954 thus becoming my uncle. Peter played lock for North Sydney (as did my father Kevin) and then went to Manly. He played two Tests for Australia in 1954–55 and played in the 1954 World Cup. The Diversis lived at Dee Why and we visited their place fairly often. Peter must have become pretty good mates with Ken Arthurson, who was then halfback at Manly, because Arko, who went on to become a heavy in administration as Manly secretary, then NSW Rugby League and Australian Rugby League chairman, is the godfather of Peter's eldest son Douglas.

I can honestly say Peter Diversi had little influence on my career. When I was younger I was a bit scared of him, maybe because he was so big and strong-looking and because he was pretty strict with the kids in his house. He ruled with an iron fist really. He's a nice enough bloke and we always get on pretty well when we see each other, but I was always a bit uncertain of him when I was a nipper. When you were at his place it was always a case of what ever he said went. And who was I to argue?

I didn't see much of Uncle Peter after my family moved west to Dundas when I was four. Dundas is between Parramatta and Carlingford, and in 1957 my parents Carley and Kevin (everyone called him Bluey) were able to find a Housing Commission home which they could buy, not just rent.

As I grew up, so did Dundas. At first there were open fields and farms, with a few fibro houses shooting up here and there. Some might say it became a bit of a rough area with Housing Commission places dominating the suburb, and for outsiders it may have been that way. To us it was simply home, where we grew up. We didn't have many luxuries, but without doubt it certainly toughened me and my attitude towards life—for the better.

Ours was a four-bedroom, fibro house. There were five kids by then: Gayle (born 1950), Michael (1951), me (1953), Marilyn (1955) and Donald (1956). All the boys lived in one room while the girls had one as well. My father had finished football by this stage but coached both League and Union for many years once we moved to Dundas. I don't know how he survived playing first grade as a lock for Norths when he weighed only 67 kg (10st 7lb). But he did and apparently he did quite well; he was something like a Paul Taylor of the '40s, snapping at the heels of his opponents and with enough pace to get around pretty well. He held a 100-yard sprint title at St Joeys so he was quicker than I ever was.

Actually sport played a pretty big role in the Price household. We were no Rhodes scholars, but we could all handle ourselves on the sporting side of things.

Dad had his football. Mum used to do a fair bit of tenpin bowling, and played with Dad on Wednesday nights. Gayle was a very good walker at school, winning a NSW title. Marilyn could have been the best of all. She used to train with June Ferguson, who was Betty Cuthbert's coach, and they thought Marilyn had as much potential as a hurdler as another girl down at Cumberland Athletics Club, Maureen Caird. But after a few years of constant trackwork, Marilyn got to the stage where the hard training became too much and she began to worry about becoming musclebound. She gave it away while Maureen Caird went on to win a gold medal at the 1968 Mexico Olympics.

For the three boys it was always Rugby Union. Union was the game at Dundas and the Dundas Valley Club, then only just formed, was for many years the stronghold of the game in the west.

We used to play at Cox Park, Carlingford. It was the Cumberland Oval of the Parramatta juniors. Other sides used to hate playing there because they reckoned it was so hard, but I loved it, just as I loved playing at Cumberland later. I didn't find either oval hard at all, just dusty. But you could tell the others were put off, and that gave us all the more incentive to slam them harder into the ground.

Michael and I started together in the under-10s; I'd just turned eight. Dad had played football and coached in the area, so it was natural that we followed, but I remember at the beginning it was more a way of getting out of church on Sunday mornings. Although we ended up playing on Saturdays, in the first few weeks there were registration days and trials on Sundays; I've only been to church for weddings and funerals since. I took up another religion on weekends.

Like a lot of kids, at the start of my football days I really didn't know what to do. All I knew was that my Dad played football, we used an oval-shaped ball, and everyone tackled. But I suppose it was in my blood. I just played the game as it came. No one ever forced me to do anything but that.

The only position I ever played in Union was breakaway. That's

Left: *Christmas 1978: Mum, Dad, Michael, Gayle, me, Marilyn, and Donald.* Below: *Even at a tender age the Prices were a sight to strike terror into the opposition. From left: Marilyn, Donald, Michael, and me in a choir boy pose.*

The learning curve: cricket at Telopea, basketball at Cumberland High, then Rugby League at Cumberland. Strangely, I always ended second from the end of the row in every team.

where I started in the under-10s. Michael was in the centres. I can still remember my first coach, Les Woods. He used to manage the Skyline drive-in theatre at North Ryde. He took us there at the end of the season for a party and we all got ice-cream cones. Alan Burts was the manager. He used to race motor cycles.

We won the competition that first year and we won plenty more at Dundas Valley, in the club that wore blue and gold just like Parramatta; gold with the two blue vees for "Valley". That first grand final was played at Oakhill College at Castle Hill, and if my memory serves me right it went into extra time against Northmead and Michael kicked the winning goal.

The only other thing I remember from that first year was playing in some sort of knockout in Manly. I dived to tackle this kid and copped his boots right in the chest. I thought I had broken every rib. I was taken off the field crying.

Strangely, I did not attain any higher representative honours in my junior football days apart from playing for the Parramatta district; although right from under-10s I made the district side every single year. My brothers and I didn't go in for school reps much either, because we had to pay to go away with the state sides and my family just couldn't afford it. And on the club scene, there were always cases of favouritism, or some kid having a father with influence. I guess that's a problem that will exist as long as sport does.

I'll never forget one year, I think it was the under-16s, when the son of the coach of the district side was hooker. There was a really hot hooker from my Dundas team who was obviously going to make the Sydney or state side. The coach—he was probably a selector as well—used plenty of influence to get his son picked as a breakaway instead. That was my position. I couldn't believe it; it really upset me. The team went to South Australia and I had set my sights on making the trip.

I realise now that that incident made me try harder to prove myself; I saw that to make anything out of life you had to do it yourself, with no favours from anyone else. Right through my career the one thing that really irked me was that no matter how much effort you put in to achieving a goal, there was always a chance of someone from outside robbing you of attaining that goal. It may have been a referee who, with a blow of the whistle, could stop you winning a grand final, or a selector who had a fancy for someone else.

Perpetual Motion

As I grew up at Dundas, football became like a drug for me. I couldn't get enough. I'd play for the school once a week, for the Valley on the weekends and just about every day after school we had a run down the road from home at the school grounds or at Acacia Park. One thing was always certain, though; it was never touch football. It was always tackle.

Quite often I'd get a run playing League on my "off" day on weekends, usually with a mate's side. In later years, when I was playing grade Union with Parramatta, I used to play League as a ring-in for Channel 9 in a Journalist's Cup competition. I used the name Vernon McGrath, who was someone else in the side who didn't turn up very often. I'm sure some of my opponents knew who I was, but no one ever squealed.

We won a heap of competitions in my years at Dundas Valley. I stayed in the under-10s the second year, still a year above myself, and we won the comp again. We won again in the under-12s two years later, then I had to "repeat" a year of under-13s to bring me back to my age group. We won the second time. I think I won four in a row from then, the last being under-18s when I was just 17.

There were some great players in those teams. But no one really kicked on. Phil Jelley played first-grade League for Parramatta, a long, blond-haired fullback in the early 1970s. Mick Bellew played grade for the Eels, and Paul Sommerville played firsts for Balmain. Plenty of others had ability, but they didn't want to let go of their mates' hands. Having a good time seemed more important than trying their guts out to be a success in football.

I still enjoyed hanging around with my mates, however. We had a pretty good life and did what I suppose most young blokes out west did: going to parties, hopping the train down to the city to a nightclub. We often used to go to a place called JCs, have a few beers and listen to the music of the time. They used to play Eagle Rock and other Daddy Cool stuff, Deep Purple, Led Zeppelin. We used to stand around having a perve like a lot of blokes. We didn't dance much.

For our group, which ranged from six to about 18 blokes, the Family Hotel on Victoria Road at Rydalmere was the regular haunt. Sometimes we'd leave at closing time, 10 pm, and decide to hop it down to Moruya on the NSW south coast or up to the Central Coast near Ettalong and Umina. We'd drive for hours, sleep in the car and then get up in the morning for a surf. A few mates had surfboards which I would occasionally ride, but body

Valley Boy

surfing was more my go. I remember once I took out a board and a big set of waves about three metres high came in and washed my board up leaving me stranded. That did me.

One time, I remember, we left the hotel at stumps and decided we'd drive down to the Snowy Mountains for the weekend. It was in the spring and there was a bit of snow still around.

They were carefree days. It was football in the winter with a few beers afterwards, and in summer it was the pub and the beach. Before we got cars, and even afterwards sometimes, we'd get the train to the city, get a ferry across to Manly and go to the beach. If we drove we'd often go to North Narrabeen or up to the Central Coast.

I wrote off my first car up at Umina; it was an old FC Holden. We were going along The Esplanade near the beach, which was still a gravel road then, and the front wheel went into a big hole, throwing the car towards a brick wall. I was speeding, trying to catch up on a mate's car in front. I swerved to miss the wall and ended up hitting one on the other side of the road, but luckily no one was hurt. That was the end of that car, which was a beauty. From then I borrowed my brother Michael's car, when he let me, until I bought a motorbike—a Honda 350. I later bought a Honda 750 which I kept for years and used to ride it to training even when I had made the Australian team.

It was a strange bunch of blokes in our group; some from football, some not. There were a few long-hairs and a couple of sharpies; sharpies and skinheads, with the crew cuts, no socks and hard-toed shoes, were around at the time, but the two in our group were pretty good blokes.

Smoking marijuana was all the go too, but I only tried it once and it did nothing for me. I often wondered what my mates saw in the stuff, and although I'd be with them when they were having a joint or two, I never again indulged. I'll never forget one mate; his nickname was Sloppy. He got six "As" in the School Certificate and was a really smart guy, but he always looked a mess. We would go around to his place when we were only about 16 or 17, and he'd have a few beers and smoke marijuana from a big bong.

I made up my own mind on those kind of things. I was always strong willed. Since I was young my upbringing had taught me one rule especially; that if you wanted something, you had to get it yourself. And don't take any notice of what everyone else was doing. I wouldn't bow to peer-group pressure.

Perpetual Motion

People never stopped telling me to get my hair cut, but the more they told me, the longer I grew it. On the other hand, if everyone had suggested politely to me that my hair needed tidying up, maybe I would have been more agreeable.

I learned quickly through my life, together with watching so many good footballers I had played with develop nothing but pot bellies in their latter years, that there was a difference between wanting something and really wanting something. You had to draw a line. You had to make sacrifices. If you weren't prepared to do that, you really didn't want to achieve it deep down.

I was a bit timid when I was young and a bit of a loner. When I was young we did the things most families did, but by the time I had reached my teens everyone had their own interests or duties. And my parents didn't get along in latter years. In 1975 they were finally divorced. But they never missed one of their sons' games of football. They were always right behind their kids when it came to sport, and they wanted the best, within their means, for the kids.

Sport is one of the best ways to build character and discipline, and it worked with our family. The kids all got on pretty well with each other, but we were all busy going our own way as well. During the week we would be off to training, and on Saturday everyone just cleared out as sport took over. There were bodies going everywhere as we all got ready for the day's events. The three boys all had separate circles of mates when we got older, but when there was a game of football on after school, it was one in, all in.

Dad won the lottery twice; well, he shared in two wins. The first time he gave up work (he was a first-class printer at Cumberland Newspapers) for 12 months and just lounged around. He bought a new car, a gold-coloured Ford, and some good furniture for the house, but the money didn't last long and he went back to work as a road sealer on the council. Not long after that, he picked up a lottery win again. Mum used to work two jobs: at Woolworths during the day and most nights in the snack bar at Parramatta Leagues Club.

My parents weren't around the house a lot, Dad was one of the many Australian men who would go to the pub after work like it was a religion. In many ways my oldest sister Gayle brought me up. She would cook the dinner and answer any problems I had, but generally I kept things inside myself. And, maybe, I still do.

I was independent. My first push bike I made myself from bits I had collected. To pick up a bit of cash I would prune roses for a guy who had a big rose garden down the road a bit. When I was old enough I started packing groceries at Coles supermarket on Thursday nights and Saturday mornings.

At school I was just an average student—"Cs" and "Ds". Maybe if I had put as much time and effort into my studies as I did with my sport I would have finished up brighter. When I left Telopea Public School I was automatically supposed to go to Cumberland High School like Gayle and Michael, but I had learned that there was no sport in first form at Cumberland so I enrolled myself at Macquarie Boys High. School fees, however, were cheaper when you had three kids from the one family at school, so I was overruled by my parents, but as it was, that year they introduced sport for first-formers at Cumberland so everything turned out apples.

The one subject I had a liking for at school was manual arts. When I left after attaining the School Certificate (I got an "A" in woodwork), I decided I wanted to be a carpenter. But everywhere I went the length of my hair came up and that was the end of it, it seemed. Mine was shoulder length, maybe a bit longer. I got so fed up with being knocked back that when I walked in for an interview at Alan Smith and Co., before Smithy could say a word I popped the first question, "Does the length of my hair have anything to do with getting this job?" He said it didn't, and then he went on to ask me his questions. I got the job as an apprentice and so my working life began, as did my weekly visits to Granville Technical College.

I was still a first year apprentice when I built in an extension underneath our home at Dundas. The house, and the extensions, and my mother are still there in Tilley Street. The house was fairly elevated, but we had to dig out below, so I used to get a few mates around, put on a carton of grog and we'd hop into it. The trouble was, though, once the grog ran out so did my mates. After six months I got it finished; I had put in two bedrooms, a lounge, a kitchenette, bathroom and toilet. Every member of the family lived downstairs when they first got married except Chris and I—we were lucky enough to have our own house.

I wasn't just a footballer and a carpenter. I used to play a fair bit of basketball and cricket when I was in my teens, although never as seriously as I played Union. I was a wicketkeeper. One day I took nine wickets—in catches and stumpings—and the manager of the other side reckoned I was going to be another Wally Grout.

But as I got older and the surf and the girls began to have more appeal, standing out in the sun for three or four hours on a Saturday was not my go. I enjoyed the few seasons I played; I used to bat at third drop and all I wanted to do was belt the cover off the ball. I picked up a few 50s and 60s for the Parramatta Leagues team. Just about all the ovals where we played had houses backing on to them, and I used to ask the manager what would happen if I broke a window. He'd think for a minute, then say, "Gee, that's a six". Each time he'd say he would pay for the damage if it happened, and each time I'd slam a six or two, but I could never break any glass.

Playing Rugby Union was always a more serious business. Curiously though, I wouldn't have known who the top Union players in Australia were because I followed League—South Sydney actually—and only stuck at Union because I started in the sport and simply enjoyed it. And Dundas Valley was a great club. Ever since I could remember, however, my intention was always to go to League.

The reason I followed the Rabbitohs was because they had a great side in the late '60s. And although every time they won a competition (in 1967-68-70-71) another club would buy up all their players, they just kept winning.

I wasn't a football groupie. I never went to Redfern to watch Souths because I was always busy playing or doing my own thing. I just took a liking to them. I used to like Bob McCarthy and John Sattler, but my favourite player was Bob Moses, he was a really tough man. Like most of Souths' good players, he ended up being bought by Manly.

Every now and then I would go down to Cumberland with my mates on a Sunday afternoon and watch the Eels, who'd lose more than they'd win in those days. When I was a bit younger I used to like watching the two Poms Ivor Lingard and Fred Pickup, and when my old friends Mick Bellew and Phil Jelley were playing for them I would pop down to see them run around. Little did I know that before too long I'd be playing at Cumberland with the big boys, and my mates would be turning up to watch me.

Union Days

I HAD NO IDEA I was going to go from Dundas under-18s straight into Parramatta first grade. It gave me a big buzz when I took the field in my initial season of grade Union, but in that first year, 1971, there was one tragic day I'll remember as long as I live. It was July 3, I was only 18 and the baby of the Parramatta Rugby Union first-grade side that took the field at Manly Oval. I was playing breakaway, and packing into the second-row, right beside me, was Lance Miller.

That day at Manly, everything turned sour. Lance Miller was tackled around the chest and hit the deck. He went down as if he was just badly winded, clutching his chest. Then he got shakily to his feet, but stumbled, and collapsed back to the ground. The next thing there was mayhem, doctors running everywhere it seemed. They came on and gave him mouth-to-mouth resuscitation, then heart massage, and then the oxygen was called for before finally they took him away in an ambulance. The game was held up for a half-hour while we all stood stunned on the field.

He never regained consciousness. That night Lance Miller was pronounced dead. He was 23, married with a child.

It was the day Evonne Goolagong became the Queen of Wimbledon, beating Margaret Court in the women's single final. It was the day when thousands of people were involved in protests in Melbourne where the South African Springboks were playing against Victoria. It was also the only day, to my knowledge, in any football code in Sydney, when a first grade footballer died from an injury on the field.

It naturally shocked everyone that a fit 23-year-old man could go like that. I don't think it has ever been made public, but it was found that the reason for his shocking death was that he was playing with pneumonia.

Apparently he had had a dose of pneumonia for a short while and no one knew. It wasn't until later that we found out it was the major cause of him becoming so distressed on the field.

It was such a sad experience. The funeral was held at the Church of England at Granville on the Tuesday, then Lance was buried at Pine Grove on the Western Highway. I remember that day, too, because the Springboks had come to Sydney and there were huge riots at the Sydney Cricket Ground where they took on the Sydney team. While the protesters were kicking up a stink about the South Africans and making front-page headlines, we were paying our last respects to a mate who just loved playing the game, politics or no politics. It certainly is a strange world.

It is a pity that the most vivid memory of my first year in Parramatta's Union ranks was such a sad one. Generally, it was an incredible first season for me.

I only went down to Parramatta because my brother Mick was already there; he had played second grade the previous season, in 1970. I expected to get a run in the under-20 colts. I couldn't believe it when I was chosen in first grade for the opening premiership match against Randwick.

The Galloping Greens were captained by one of Union's all-time greats, Ken Catchpole, a legend of a halfback and Australian captain in 13 Tests. Randwick also had a scraggy blond-haired fullback who could kick a few goals. His name was Russell Fairfax.

I was pretty cocky about being in first grade and I was always a pretty aggressive sort of footballer, so naturally I thought I'd see how good this legend Catchpole was. To put it bluntly, I thought I'd belt him every chance I got. Catchpole was about 32 by then, a short, nuggety guy. In the first ruck Randwick won, I lined him up and clouted him. He got the ball away first and I was following play across field when I felt a "thump" across my head from behind. As I've looked up, this giant was just jogging past. I had no idea who he was. All I heard was a really deep voice say, "Leave him alone".

I was a pretty persistent young bloke and, as I said, aggressive and pretty cocky. So I ignored the advice and a couple of rucks later, I gave Catchpole another one. The same thing happened. A big bloke, and I can't remember who he was, bashed me again. "I told you to leave him alone," he growled.

After a third such incident I decided that these blokes had been at the game longer than me, and maybe they knew what they were

Union Days

talking about. I certainly learned one thing that day: in Rugby Union the greats are looked after by their own and they don't take kindly to young upstarts trying to make a quick name for themselves. Funnily enough, towards the end of my Rugby League career I started to share the same attitude after a few mugs would occasionally try to take a cheap shot at one of the top players. Like me back in 1971, usually they would soon realise they couldn't replace experience with cockiness.

I must admit, though, that during most of my Union days I loved trying to cut down the tall poppies. I was aggressive to the extent that I sailed pretty close to the wind with the rules, and when I see old film of my Union days, I realise just how "aggro" I was. But I wasn't the biggest bloke in the game. In fact you could call me a bit scrawny—and the only way to survive was to show I had no fear.

Another game I'll never forget was the match against Drummoyne at Drummoyne Oval in 1973. It was Greg Davis's farewell match in Australia before he moved to New Zealand. Davis, who later died from cancer in New Zealand, was about 33 or 34, and regarded as one of Australia's greatest breakaways. I virtually succeeded him as the regular breakaway in the Australian team.

There had been a heap of publicity about Davis' big farewell game and a big crowd turned up. I thought I would give him a farewell he would never forget, so I played as aggressively as I could and never stopped hounding Davis. I probably went too far and next thing, a big right hand came out of nowhere in a ruck and thumped me. I retaliated and all of a sudden there was an all-in brawl. It seemed as though I was fighting the whole Drummoyne pack. They wanted to kill me. It caused one of the biggest stirs in Sydney Rugby Union.

I have rarely been so cranky. I was the only player sent off, dismissed for fighting, but I certainly wasn't fighting myself. There was a furore in the papers the next day: "Punching broke out frequently ... it was a vicious, spiteful game," was one of the comments.

Davis took it like the champion he was and simply said, "It was one of those things, arms were going everywhere." And he said it with a smile. That day reminded me of the old westerns on television; it didn't really matter who was the quickest on the draw, the good guys always won.

That first year I played six games in reserves and 12 in firsts. By the end of the season I had established myself. I ended up playing 68 first grade games for the Two Blues, most of them with Michael and quite a few with Donald in my last season, 1975.

Parramatta wasn't one of the top clubs in 1971, but we had some pretty good young players plus a few old hands like Alan Minnett, the big prop. Big Al was like a Mick Cronin to the young guys. Short hair, clean cut, tough but always fair. He had been in first grade nearly a decade when I arrived. Minnett never stopped trying and he led by example. I was the youngest in the side and I always thought that if he could keep going so should I.

Big Al went through plenty of lean years with Parramatta; he must have been around as many seasons as his League counterpart Bob O'Reilly. But unlike the Bear, Minnett never tasted victory on grand-final day. When Parra finally made it to the big one in 1974 and 1975, he finished a loser. Minnett is now the Parramatta club secretary. Another guy in Parramatta firsts when I came in was Ivor Mann, long-serving forward who played 284 first grade games. He was one of the Manns, a famous Parramatta footballing family. And there were Tony Herring, Doug Walter, Peter Wheeler, NSW centre Rick Andrews, Paddy Cooper, and Greg Hackett. Doug Walter was nothing like famous cricketer Doug Walters in appearance. He was a big man, but he had a similar down-to-earth nature and was a keen punter. He would bet on anything.

Our coach was Rod Phelps, whom I always regarded as somewhat of a Jack Gibson of Rugby Union. Phelps was a dentist who had a practice at Wentworthville for years and years and still has. He was a quiet type of person, very articulate, and he never yelled to get his point across, but, like Gibbo, he had an aura of respectability and authority about him. And he was always interested in his players off the field.

Many times he would have a party at his place for the team; he'd always supply the food and drink himself. We drank out of pewter mugs he had collected over the years, many of them presented to him during his own football-playing days and inscribed for some or other award. We were really impressed; he wasn't just a coach who had all the theories, but was quite a brilliant player himself. He played centre and fullback for Australia. Those parties always showed he cared for his players, and I thought then, if I became a coach, it was something I would like to do.

In those days, if you played representative Rugby you missed plenty of club games, which always went ahead as scheduled. So

Opposition forwards, most of them a lot bigger than me, were always sizing me up. In this case it was two Randwick forwards in a Rugby Union match at North Sydney Oval.

The Parramatta Rugby Union side of 1972 with my brother Michael second on the left in the middle row and me second on the right in the front row. Coach Rod Phelps (far right, back row) taught me a lot about football and was one of the few people at Parramatta Rugby Union Club to accept my switch to League.

the only time I played anywhere near the full complement of games for Parramatta was in 1972, putting in 19 appearances. I played 13 in 1973 because of a couple of injuries, but in those first two full years in first grade, despite many critics claiming I should have had a run in the representative teams, I never got a look in.

It was much the same as my first two seasons in Rugby League, but it never really worried me because I was purely concentrating on establishing myself in first grade. If higher honours came, it was a bonus. And I've always thought that the major aim of any footballer should be to be consistent at first-grade level. Some players have purple patches and play for Australia. Others have a meteoric rise but then can't keep the momentum going. The real test of a sportsman is his ability to perform consistently well over a long period, and fortunately I think I achieved that.

The 1972 season was tremendous for me because I became one of the youngest players ever to win the Fairfax Cup for the competition's best and fairest. I was involved in a ding-dong battle with a few players, including Gordon halfback Rex Batterham and Port Hacking's Keith Halpin. With one round remaining, I had it wrapped up, and naturally it was a fantastic thrill at 19 years of age. I didn't poll any points in the last round and ended up two clear of Halpin, who picked up two points, and three clear of Batterham and Eric Tindall from Drummoyne.

Actually, looking over the records I found I fared pretty well in the Fairfax Medal over quite a few seasons, although I never went close to winning it again. In 1973 I finished equal fourth, five points behind Wayne Florentine from Manly (Russell Fairfax came equal second) and in 1974, when I only played 14 matches, I finished equal third, four points behind the winner, Bruce Buchan, from Port Hacking.

It wasn't until that year that I was recognised by the selectors. It was also the year Parramatta played in their first grand final since 1945 and only the club's second since entering the competition in 1934. I had been chosen in a Probables versus Possibles match which was used as a Wallaby trial in 1972. (I was picked as a reserve and didn't even get a run.) Then, at the start of 1973, I was picked in a Sydney training squad and played against Combined Services. But I didn't get a real sniff of the action until 1974, and just as it would be for me in League, once I got the scent of the representative stuff I just had to have more.

The Sydney team went to Melbourne to play in a Wallaby

Trophy match against Victoria; that was the start of it all for me. After that, Sydney played The Rest in a selection trial; we won 26-12 and I picked up a try. By then, apparently, I was starting to be seen as a Test possible.

I don't know why there was such a sudden change. Maybe, before then, a rough-house, long-haired bikie from Dundas didn't fit the tweed coat, Mercedes Benz image of Rugby Union. That was until they needed a bit of aggression in the pack, and suddenly I was okay. Maybe I just had to serve an apprenticeship in the selectors' eyes. I don't know.

If there was a class syndrome in Rugby Union, it went over my head at the time. Footballers were footballers to me; we were all made of the same stuff. We all bled the same. I was aware that some of the guys I played with were from wealthy backgrounds, but it didn't affect me; I didn't feel inferior. Sport is a great leveller. I suppose it used to make them look when I turned up to representative training in an army coat on my motorbike, but the players always treated me as just one of the team. There was always a lot of mutual respect.

My next rep game was for Sydney against a pretty good Country side that beat us. Country had plenty of internationals in those days, which are seen now as a bit of a golden era for the boys from the bush. On the 1975-76 Wallaby tour there were Greg Cornelsen, skipper John Hipwell, John Lambie, Stuart MacDougall, John Weatherstone, Glen Eisenhauer, Peter Horton and Brian Mansfield all from the sticks.

I went into the NSW side for the first time, and after a pretty rugged game against Queensland at Ballymore, the newspapers were saying I was a good chance to play in the Tests against the All Blacks. I remember that first NSW team I played in: Laurie Monaghan, Owen Stephens, John Weatherstone, Geoff Shaw, John Cole, John Berne, John Hipwell (c), myself, Tony Gelling John Lambie, Garrick Fay, Roger Davis, Lars Hedberg, Peter Horton, Stuart MacDougall.

It was a really tough game against the Queenslanders. They beat us 7-6. Garrick Fay had 20 stitches inserted behind his ear and I came off with a shoulder injury. I started pouring the ice treatment into it straight away because there was no way I was going to miss the Sydney versus All Blacks game. I played, but the All Blacks beat us 33-10 even though our forwards stood up to them pretty well. Then NSW came up against the New Zealanders and we were beaten 20–0. Unfortunately I thought some of our forwards turned it up a bit that day, and it only made me want to have another crack at the All Blacks even more.

Then, finally, the news came: I'd made the Australian side. I was just 21. The Test selectors had made sweeping changes with six players turning out for their Test debuts—myself, Victorian John Meadows, Peter Horton, John Lambie, Roger Davis, and Paul McLean. The team was Monaghan, Cole, David L'Estrange, Shaw, Jeff McLean, Paul McLean, Hipwell, Price, Mark Loane, Fay, Davis, Meadows, Horton, MacDougall.

Australia had only beaten the All Blacks once since 1958, and that was 10 years before that current season, in 1964. But we had some young and keen players and we were ready to give the world champions something to think about. For me, as well, there was a great honour in playing for Australia, because I became Parramatta's first international since Eric Tweedale in 1946.

I'll never forget my first Test match. It was at the Sydney Cricket Ground. Everyone I knew from Dundas Valley and Parramatta went to the game and sat on the Hill. It was a bog and it rained persistently the whole game. And it was freezing. But we really took it to the All Blacks in the forwards and, although we went down 11–6, we were in the match all the way.

The greatest moment for me was scoring a try in my Test debut. It's a treasured memory. Paul McLean had a shot at goal and the ball hit the post, rebounded and I regathered and slid over in the left-hand corner right in front of my family and friends on the Hill. I looked up and saw them all standing up cheering. And then someone raised a big banner which said, "The Ray Price Stand". Magic!

A draw would have been a good result in that first Test, but at least we headed for Ballymore convinced we could give the All Blacks a run for their money. In the second Test we did draw 16-all, but as far as I was concerned we were robbed—by our "own" referee. Bob Burnett gave us a caning all match, then to top it off he ruled double-movement when Geoff Shaw scored what we all claimed was a dead-set try. At least the public and the press got right behind the Australian side. We had won plenty of friends for our wholehearted efforts in coming back from 16–6.

All the heart went out of the third Test. Some of our pack didn't get into their work at all and we went down 16–6. We didn't cross their line; our two goals came from Paul McLean. That was also the day my special tackle, the "Cumberland throw", started to cause a bit of a stir. The All Blacks weren't too keen on me hurling them over my leg, but as far as I and the referee were concerned, it was completely legal—and a pretty convincing way for someone my size to hurt the big fellas. It was a tackle that I first saw when Ivor Lingard and Fred Pickup, two Poms who played for Parramatta League, used it in the late 1960s. You had to pick the right time and the right angle, but when you got them with a Cumberland throw they knew it.

That was the end of the rep stuff for me that season. It was back to Parramatta. And, back on the club scene, it was great being part of that club's revival. After being also-rans for so long we came in minor premiers in 1974, ahead of Randwick.

Looking over the press clippings, I realise just what a big part my brother Michael played in our success. Quite often he would score just about all our points in tries and goals, and I used to pick up quite a few "meat pies" myself back in those days.

We virtually wrapped up the minor premiership thanks to one of the strangest ploys I've ever seen in my football career. It happened in the second-last game of the year, against Gordon. They had blitzed us late in the game to score two tries and come back to 17-16 right on the bell. Their goalkicker, Malcolm Jack, lined up the conversion from not far to the right of the post. It certainly wasn't a difficult kick, but in Rugby Union you were allowed to charge the kicker when he was taking conversions. Jack was just taking his last step back when our prop, Mick Bull, tore out and just before Jack got to the ball, Bull belted it off its mound.

Jack didn't know what had hit him. He was stunned. It scared the hell out of him. The referee ruled that Jack had a free kick at goal—we weren't allowed to try to charge it down. So he gently lined it up again, connected, and the ball hit the left post. No goal. Parramatta had won and went on to take the minor premiership by one point.

There was only one stranger thing I have seen on a football field, and that was the next season when Sydney played Country. It is referred to now as the infamous "ball up the jumper" trick. It was a special move which was the brainchild of Country's coach Darryl Haberecht. I think they called it "Tap 5" and they used it against Sydney at the T.G. Milner Field in the last two minutes. I was one of the dummies who fell for it.

Country got a penalty about 40 metres out from our line and their skipper John Hipwell decided to take a tap kick. All the other players went in a semi-circle around him and turned their backs to us. Then so did Hipwell. I remember a few of the Sydney players looking at each other thinking what the hell was going on. Next thing, Hipwell took the tap and players scattered in all directions, every one of them with both arms crossed under their jumpers. We just had no idea who had the ball.

We just went for whoever we suspected, and before we realised Greg Cornelson had the ball tucked under his jumper, he'd got a break on us. The chase was on, but Cornelson slipped the ball to big second-rower Brian Mansfield who plunged over in the corner. You wouldn't believe it: Jim Hindmarsh kicked the conversion from right near touch and Country won the flamin' game.

I think Country tried the ploy against England that year, but it didn't come off. And on the Wallaby tour later that year the Australian side tried it at least once. But the referee wouldn't allow it; it was "against the spirit of the game, old chum".

Grand-final day inexperience, and extra time in two earlier games, went a long way towards Parramatta failing to pull off a fairytale in 1974.

It was the club's first grand final in my lifetime and after so many years in the doldrums, the whole club was alive with expectation. We had beaten the mighty Randwick in the minor semi-final 9–3, and went into Parramatta's second grand final in its 40-year history. That semi-final win was Parramatta's first win against Randwick since 1962, when big prop Alan Minnett and our coach Rod Phelps had played.

The team met at the licensed club at Westmead late in the morning and we all took off in a bus for the Sydney Sports Ground. But when we got there, everything was out of kilter. Both the third and fourth grades had had to play 20 minutes extra time each. We arrived at the ground pretty early, but ended up sitting around sweating it out for what seemed an eternity. By the time we ran out for the first-grade grand final, 54 minutes late, the tension was showing.

Randwick, who had had plenty of experience on grand-final day, had rung up earlier in the day. They'd found out the games were behind schedule and altered their arrival time at the ground accordingly. We didn't have such foresight, and had virtually no

Union Days

grand-final experience between us. In fact, our centre Rick Andrews and Minnett were the only ones who could have been called seasoned.

Randwick had got on top before we'd regained any sort of composure. They scored a try when they charged down a kick by our fullback Bruce Coggins inside our own quarter, regathered and touched down. It was 6–3 at halftime, but we really hadn't played well. Randwick went to 10–3 in the second half and were always going to win. Brother Michael put Warren Robbiliard over for a try right near the end and Mick kicked the conversion after the siren had sounded to make it just one point difference, 10–9. I really reckon that had the game not started so late and put us off our preparation, we would have won that grand final.

There is nothing worse than being a loser on grand-final day. It is a hollow feeling. The other team do their victory lap and get all the congratulations. The losers stand there like shags on a rock. Second best doesn't count. There are the winners and the rest. When you look in the record books later only the premiers get their names listed. They are the only ones the people remember.

We were pretty proud that we had taken the club to greater heights than it had been used to, but I've never been able to accept losing, nor gain much satisfaction from it. Unfortunately, it was a feeling I got used to. It was the first of four successive years in which I was in a team who played bridesmaids. I played in three successive grand-final losses, all by three points or less, before I got a draw in 1977 on Rugby League's historical day. It was the game's first drawn grand final, between Parramatta and St George, but a week later we went down 22–0 in the replay, a match that should never have been played.

In 1975, Parramatta Union went through to the grand final first again, after beating minor premiers, Randwick. The 'Wicks then got flogged by Northern Suburbs 22–3 in the final, but we still thought this was the day the Two Blues were going to get the Shute Shield.

We were stronger in 1975, I thought. Many of the younger players, including myself, were a bit more experienced. Rod Batterham, an international three-quarter who was approaching the end of his career, joined us from Gordon, adding some much needed experience in the backline. Plus he was a topline left-footed goalkeeper who took over the reins from Michael, who had shown to be pretty top-class himself.

Perpetual Motion

There wasn't a try scored in that grand final, which we lost 9-6 on penalty goals. Norths' Allen Anderson potted a penalty goal from about 40 metres with two minutes to go. I couldn't believe it. Anderson ended up kicking three goals from five attempts; Batters landed only two from five. That was the ball game. Although the Norths' forwards, led by their skipper and Test player Reg Smith, were too big and strong on the day, we should have won. We actually got over their line, but dropped the ball. Michael had made a break and threw the ball to Rick Andrews, who centre kicked. My breakaway partner, Peter Thompson, got to the ball first, but knocked it on over the line in a mad scramble.

Accepting defeat was even harder knowing it was Alan Minnett's last game. He had played 272 first-grade games for the club and tried his guts out in every one of them. At that stage he was third in the all-time list of Rugby Union survivors in the Sydney competition. Only Manly's prop Tony Miller, who played for a generation in 345 games, and another Parramatta veteran Ivor Mann (284 games) had played more first grade matches.

Little did anyone know at the time but it was also my last game for the club. I had quite a few beers that night knowing that it was probably the case. Losing the grand final ruined what otherwise was a great season for me which had been capped off with my selection in the Wallaby team to tour Britain. My intention was always to switch to League, so I more or less had planned that the grand final was my last game for the Two Blues. Then I would play in all Tests on the tour and come back to League. Things did not go according to plan.

The 1975 Australian season was probably my best; Parramatta had again made a grand final and I had finally established myself as one of Australia's top Test players. It's strange how you get more liberties as you become more accepted. When I first made the rep stuff in 1974, you had to pass the team medical early in the week or be ruled unfit. I had plenty of nagging injuries during my Union days, but by 1975 I would be picked when there was no chance of passing a medical and I'd be given until sometimes the day of the match to prove I was right.

We won all four Tests at home in '75, two against England and two against Japan in the only series ever played against that nation. What were the Japs like? Well I'm not trying to be funny, but they were nippy. There was no size about them, which made life fairly easy in the line-outs, but they could dance around the

Union Days

field, much like the Fijian sides of recent times. In many ways it was like touch football. We won the first Test 37-7 in Sydney and the second 50-25 in Brisbane. The scores against England that year were 16-9 in Sydney, then 30-21 in Brisbane.

The Poms played the game pretty hard, but weren't too impressed with the physical way our forwards got into them. You could say we put them off their game. They had one forward called Mike Burton, who was sent off in a very fiery second Test at Ballymore. The Poms claimed afterwards he was madly provoked, and I have to concede we baited him a bit. And they had a second-rower called Billy Beaumont; just about every match he played on tour he came off with blood splattered everywhere. Everyone got stuck into him whether it was in a Test or games against state or provincial sides.

We had some pretty tough bunnies in those days, guys like Stuart MacDougall, Peter Horton and Steve Finnane. In a book he released years later, Mike Burton didn't have too many kind words to say about us, myself included. That's football!

Actually the Poms were a disappointment on that tour, but traditionally they haven't played well in Australia. The hard grounds and touring lifestyle don't seem to suit them. Their League teams have been the same in the era since 1971.

That rugged Test in Brisbane ended up being my last in Rugby Union. I had made the Wallabies, but the tour was virtually a disaster for me as a player. Yet I still have fond memories of my last season as a rah rah. Little (I should say younger) brother Donald, Michael and I played together in a few first-grade games that season. Donald was 19 and in his first season with Parramatta. He has slowly developed since then, playing mostly lock, and went on to become an international against Fiji in 1980, another family achievement of which we are very proud. That first season he played most of his first-grade games as my replacement while I was on representative duty.

Michael never represented but he proved a consistent and valuable first-grader for seven seasons before he followed me to League in 1978.

Donald also continued the family trend by switching to League in 1982; he went to Penrith where he played two seasons. Neither of my brothers ever played regular first grade in League, which was a great pity. Mick scored a lot of points in reserve grade where he played on the wing and won a competition in 1979. Donald, I thought, was a little harshly done by. I think he was under-rated and didn't get the opportunity he deserved. He switched to Parramatta in 1984, but didn't play much in firsts. He backed up the next season and then retired, but after a year out he decided, aged 30, to trial for a spot at Parramatta again and was graded as a prop in 1987.

It is always hard following in the shadows of someone else in the family. Although Michael was older, both he and Donald had to do that when they switched to League, but I will always regard them as above average footballers in their own right and the three of us have all been inspiration to each other during our careers.

On The Wallaby Tour

BECOMING A WALLABY was one of my goals after playing all seven Tests at home in 1974 and '75. And it was one of my proudest achievements. But while getting into the Wallaby squad might have been something, getting to England was another kettle of fish.

I had been outside Australia once before, when Parramatta had a tour of New Zealand at the end of 1974; in Dunedin I was billeted out with three young women, with me being the only man in the house. It was unbelievable. The British tour, however, was to be my first real trip overseas.

In the months before I left, Rod Phelps often had me over at his place tutoring me on the finer things in life, explaining what to expect on tour. We drank wine, I learned which fork and knife was for what. He educated and prepared me. The trouble was, we nearly didn't make it to the British Isles. One newspaper said we were lucky not to be all killed, and that was only on the way over.

I was young and keen and it was a big thing for me to be going overseas. After a few beers I'd settled down on the plane; first stop was Hong Kong and the plane was packed. Luckily most of the passengers were Asian and they piled off at Honkers. We thought that was great, because we'd then have a bit of room to stretch out and take it easy. Bull!

Apparently a cyclone was moving towards Hong Kong from the sea. We landed without any worries; the stopover was to be an hour, but while we were hanging around, there was talk that we might have to stay a lot longer because of the cyclone.

The pilot decided we'd take off and head away from the coast towards the mountains to get away from the cyclone, so we all piled on, up we went and before I knew it, I looked out the window and I saw a big red flame shoot right past me. It's funny, the first thing

I thought of was how lucky it was that Stuart MacDougall, who was sitting across from me, was looking the other way. He couldn't handle flying at the best of times, and would have fainted quick smart if he had seen that fire.

The plane dropped about 20 feet and we all thought that it was going to crash, and if it wasn't for the quick thinking of the pilot, I reckon it would have. He gave the plane full throttle, gunned it, then banked around the front of a range of mountains. We came so close to them that when I looked out the window it felt as if you could have touched them if you put out your hand. It was scary.

The panic died down and the pilot announced we would have to detour to Singapore because of "engine trouble". You beauty, we thought, that would be the end of that. Then, bugger me, we were just coming down to land at Singapore when we blew another engine. Singapore must have one of the biggest runways in the world because we just kept going and going and going. Finally the plane came to a halt and you should have seen the look on Runt's (MacDougall's) face.

It was announced we would have to stop over in Singapore for 24 hours while the engines were checked. No worries, at least we were safe. Or so I thought. We lobbed into Singapore airport with no luggage; nothing but the clothes we had on. Then someone grabbed me and reminded me there were hair restrictions in this joint—nothing below the collar. I was only over the limit by about a foot.

I tucked the locks into my collar and thought I should be all right. My team-mates had just about all gone through customs when an official grabbed me by the arm and all hell broke loose. They weren't going to let me into the country. Fortunately the team manager, Ross Turnbull, intervened and explained that it was not our fault we had to stop over in Singapore, that we were only staying for one night, and they'd keep me out of the way. Luckily, the airport authorities agreed. I'm glad, because there was no way I was going to get my hair cut.

We finally made it to England 60 hours after we left Sydney. And we'd been in our uniforms the whole time. Believe me, some of us were starting to smell a bit "woofee".

That wasn't the end of the saga though. We'd been booked to go to the Australian Embassy for a function and it was too late to get out of it, so we threw our bags in the room, those who had to shave did (I had no worries) and wearing the same stinking clothes we piled into a bus and went off to the embassy. What a start to the tour.

While I still remember it was a magnificent experience, the tour didn't get much better for me. I played only six games, spent nine days in hospital and almost got sent home because of a smart-alec Scotsman.

After the third game on tour, a match against Ulster, I thought I had broken a finger. The next day we headed to Scotland for a game against Edinburgh, so I thought I'd get it checked out. I was sitting in the waiting room of the Scottish team doctor's surgery and second-rower Glen Eisenhauer was sitting next to me, waiting to have his sore ribs checked out flicking through a medical magazine. He leaned across and said, "Have a go at this, Pricey. Look at the size of this bloke's balls; they're bigger than my football bag."

There was a photo of a poor bloke who had a hernia. I took the magazine off him and had a look through. I was nice and swollen from a kick I had got against the All Blacks the season before. I glanced through the article, thinking to myself that some of the symptoms seemed familiar. When I went in to see about my finger I just casually asked the doctor to check me out down below, just in case I had a hernia.

He fiddled around, looked up at me and told me I was right. And what's more, he reckoned that if I got a bad kick in the scrotum I could be killed because of what he called strangulation. Bloody hell.

The doctor recommended I get into hospital the next day and have the hernia repaired. He told me I'd be in hospital for seven days and I'd be right to play in four or five weeks. The tour was only young and we had nearly three months to go, so I did what the doctor ordered.

The Five Nations, an organisation which ran the international Rugby affairs of England, France, Scotland, Wales and Ireland, volunteered to foot the medical bill and decided I could stay in Edinburgh. They were to meet the hotel costs as well and I could catch up with the team when they came back for the Test against Scotland. So in I went for the operation. There were no dramas, and I remember the next day I was a little uncomfortable so I hopped out of bed to go for a leak. The nurse went off her brain, yelling at me that I wasn't suppose to be walking around and that I could do some serious damage.

After a few days it was really giving me the dirts. All my teammates were out playing around the counties and there I was sitting in bloody hospital. Then the parents of the kid across from me decided to have him, at the tender age of 17, circumcised. He was squealing day and night; I felt like belting him. And what made it worse was that everyone else was getting visitors. There I was, a long way from home, alone. I had to get out of the place.

The surgeon finally lobbed in after a couple of days. He told me the operation was spot on, everything was great, I'd be out of the joint in another week (that made it 10 days from the operation) and I'd be right to play in six to eight weeks. What? Before I could protest that he had told me earlier I'd be out within a week after the operation and playing in five, he was on his way out of the room, so I got up and chased him, and started abusing him as I romped after him through the wards. You should have seen that old nurse.

As it turned out, I had the stitches out on the ninth day, I left the hospital and returned to our hotel the day before the fellas got back for the Test. Next day I started walking; once I was well enough I started jogging, and four weeks to the day after the operation I was back on the paddock for the game against Cornwall and Devon. A Welsh doctor cleared me. I'd missed the Test against Scotland (we lost 10-3) and the Test against Wales (we lost 28-3). I had some catching up to do. At least there were the Tests against England and Ireland to come.

In my second game back—against Combined Services—that bloke upstairs got me again. About 15 minutes into the game I was going across in cover and I dived at a bloke from the side. Somehow my hand went through his legs between his stride, came up and went whack; my thumb broke. It didn't break the skin, but you could see the bone protruding out. I stayed down and the physio came on. I told him, "Don't you dare say a word to anyone. Just strap it up and leave me on." I finished the game with no one else knowing, but I could tell I'd broken the bastard. We went back to the barracks and I got it X-rayed. There was a clean break and I had to have it operated on.

I missed another five games, including two Tests, then made myself available for the clash with Munster, which I played. I also made myself available for the last game in Britain, the "Test" against the Barbarians, which is always a big affair, but the selectors reckoned I wasn't match fit and they passed me by.

On the Wallaby Tour

So that was it—six bloody games. On the way home we played an unofficial Test against the United States in Los Angeles, but I had missed all the Tests in Britain. Being so far from home for the first time and having such rotten luck made it a pretty tough experience. It was costly too. It was my right thumb I had broken, so I couldn't write any letters; the hand was good enough to dial the telephone though, and that's where most of my £2 daily allowance went, although my mother will dob me in and claim I reversed the charges most of the time.

Despite the hard times, any Wallaby tour still provides some incredible memories and some funny stories. Rugby Union, particularly in Britain, is real upper class, plum-in-the-mouth stuff. And anyone who knows this boy from Dundas will tell you he doesn't fit into that sort of social circle. After each game we'd go to a function where every dignitary in town would turn up. I'm sure I was looked upon as some sort of freak, with my scraggy beard and hair halfway down my back. But I didn't care; I just acted myself.

Only once did I get into any sort of bother. It was at a function after the Test against Scotland. I had only been out of hospital a few days and there was a bit of publicity about the hernia. At this "do", one of the Scottish officials who was half-full of ink asked me if he could see my scar. After he wouldn't give in—he kept telling me he was just curious because he'd never seen a hernia scar before—I undid my zipper, nudged down the strides and said "There ya go". You wouldn't believe it, but he threw his drink down my pants; he thought it was a big joke. I was going to kill him, and it took Ron Graham, Peter Horton and Ross Turnbull all their strength to hold me back.

Next day I had to report to Turnbull, the manager. He got me in and started talking about sending me home. We had a pretty lively man-to-man talk and thrashed it out. I was staying.

Mostly, those get togethers, and the company in general, provided some incredibly funny memories. Union is seen as rather toffy, and certainly there were some blokes on the tour with "poshy" backgrounds. Compared to a Rugby League tour, it's all classy stuff over there. We stayed at the Waldorf Hotel in London, one of the city's more elegant places; all our laundry, food and more often than not the drinks, were paid for. The 1975 League World Cup side was over there at the same time—staying at some dingy hotel.

Perpetual Motion

But my team-mates on tour were just like me. They loved a bit of fun, didn't mind a drink, and gave their all when it came to football. And anyone who has Stuart (Runt) MacDougall and John Lambie with them has to enjoy themselves. They were two of the funniest guys I've ever met, and it was just laughs all the time with that pair. Every morning Runt would get on the bus and make the announcement: "Right, I'm unavailable unless selected. Are there any press here, did you hear that?"

Christmas Eve was a crazy night. MacDougall's wife was in England at the time and he had been skiting all day about what he'd be up to that night while we'd be hanging around the hotel. A lot of the guys were out for Christmas; those who wanted to spend it with a family were billetted. There were about half of us left when MacDougall lobbed downstairs ready to meet his wife wherever she was staying. He thought he was the ant's pants. We had organised a fancy-dress party at the hotel, but before he left Runt gave out his Christmas presents. He had a nappy for Ken Wright, the baby of the side at 19, and there was one of those T-shirts with a set of boobs on it for someone else.

We had booked one of the long tables at the Waldorf for Christmas dinner and before too long it looked like a bit of a pig sty. We were having a great time singing Christmas carols, but a group on the other side of the room weren't impressed and complained about us. We were only trying to have a good time and when you're a long way from family and friends that's the only way to beat the frustration. So we thought bugger 'em; a few of us got up, walked over to their table and started singing carols to them like a Spanish quartet serenading a couple of lovers in a romantic restaurant. Didn't they have the shits.

David Brockhoff, who coached Sydney University in the Sydney competition, was the Australian coach on that Wallaby tour. He was also my NSW coach right through my international Union career, taking over the Test side from Queenslander Bob Templeton who was my first national coach in 1974.

You'd swear blind he played every match with us, made every tackle, and was in every ruck. Brockhoff would wear his official uniform to every match, but by the time the game had finished he would have broken out in a lather of sweat and was so hyped up it was incredible. He would be so exhausted, he'd go back to the hotel, go up to his room, take off his good clobber and put on his tweed pants, cream jumper and slippers, sit in his chair, put on

Michael (left), Donald (centre) and myself at the old Cumberland Oval in our Rugby Union Days with Parramatta. Long hair may have been the fashion in those days, but it was to create problems for me on the way to England with the 1975 Wallabies.

The 1975 Wallabies had a great tour of England, but it was a tough time for me with plenty of injury problems.

some soft music and stay there for at least a good half-hour before anyone saw him.

Brockhoff had an incredible turn of phrase and some great sayings. Whenever NSW played at Ballymore, he always referred to "Sharks in muddy water" and one of his favourites was "You know you've got the game by the throat when you hear the turnstiles clicking as the Queenslanders are leaving". He had some magic words for every occasion. He was a very good coach, and a very well spoken and intelligent man who fitted in well with the social set we continually mixed with while on tour. He was a great speaker with a terrific knowledge on a wide range of topics.

We attended function after function and met a lot of famous people. One night at the Savoy, in London, every "big nob" in town was there, including Douglas "Tin Legs" Bader. We had a chat with him for a while; he was there with two walking sticks telling us how he'd just finished 18 holes of golf!

The best night by far was when we went to Buckingham Palace to meet the Queen. We had to go to a place outside the palace first and make sure every button was right, every wrinkle ironed, and every hair in place. I had my hair cut for the occasion; actually, putting it into perspective, the Queen is the only person I have ever had my hair cut for. While we were in Liverpool one of the players was hanging around with a local lass who was a hairdresser, so I got her to give me a royal haircut. We went up to the player's room, I just can't remember who he was, off came about six inches and she tidied it up and layered it on top. To this day I reckon it's the best haircut I've ever had.

While we were in the room outside the palace with me looking tidier than I had ever been, we were briefed on what to say when Queen Elizabeth greeted us and how to behave ourselves. We were all very nervous. Unfortunately for some of us, the lesson didn't go too far.

Then we got to the palace and we walked up the stairs, with everyone going through in their minds what they had to say and do. We had to wait in a big hallway hung with beautiful big paintings. They were the Real McCoys; no copies. I've never seen anything like it in my life. All the furniture was antique, and there was gold etching right around the cornices. Unbelievable!

We then proceeded to a big conference room where the Queen, Princess Anne and Prince Charles met us. There were packets of Buckingham Palace cigarettes, specially marked ash trays, the lot.

On the Wallaby Tour

There were "souvenirs" being loaded into pockets everywhere. The Queen was only supposed to be with us for 40 minutes, but she stayed two hours. I think she enjoyed herself.

Apparently a few of the guys were chatting with her when Trash Can (that's Norm Tasker, then a journo from the *Sydney Sun*) asked her if she followed the Rugby match. "Oh yes," she replied. "I've been following your fortunes. How's that young man with the long hair getting on since his unfortunate injury?"

They called me over to introduce me to her. It was a bit of a shock and after all the coaching I'd had I still got a bit of stage fright. "Ray, please meet Her Majesty the Queen."

I thought "Shit!" Then I said, "Um, g'day. How are ya?" All that etiquette training went down the drain in one fell swoop.

A bit later we were having a chat to Prince Charles. Lambie was not trying to be smart (although you never know) when he was talking to him about how tough it must have been to be such a public figure. "You wouldn't be able to slip down the pub for a few ales with the boys, would you, Charles?" Lambie asked. "And I suppose you'd have to be careful if you wanted to take a bird out?"

Charles was great. Whatever question we asked, he answered. We were totally fascinated. And he said to Lambie, "Yes it is a bit difficult. You've got to be able to trust your close friends. And, actually, I do sneak down and have a couple of ales."

Just about then MacDougall rocked up to him and slipped his business card into Charles' top suit pocket. MacDougall and his family owned Stanley Wines. "Listen Charlie," he said, "There's my card, next time you're down in Sydney look us up and I'll take you for a night up the Cross." Charles asked what was at the Cross. "Well for starters I'll fix you up with a sheila and we'll have a few beers," Runt said. It brought the house, or should I say the palace, down.

The Switch

IT WAS A LONG flight home from Los Angeles. We had stopped there on the way home from Britain to play an unofficial Test against America, and fighting fit after all the dramas of the tour, I played in that historic match. I started to wonder if it would be my last Union match or not.

Before I had left for Britain I'd more or less decided it was the time to switch to League. Mark Loane, who was pretty close to me, knew. The others? Well, they knew I was thinking of changing. There had been a fair bit in the papers about me turning to League and for a while I thought I wouldn't be chosen for the Wallaby tour because of the reports.

The media can be cruel, as I found even more in later years. But there was one media man I grew to know and like very much on tour, good old Trash Can Norm Tasker. We had some great nights together. I respected him as a journo and got on well with him as a bloke. It's strange that 12 years down the road we came together again when Norm took over as managing editor at *Rugby League Week* where I have enjoyed doing a column for five years.

All sorts of things were going through my mind on that flight home. John White, a good family friend and more or less my adviser in those days, had sounded out a few clubs on my behalf—Balmain, Canterbury and, of course, Parramatta. He had kept me in touch with happenings while I had been away, but by the time the tour was over, I was having second thoughts. I had had such a disappointing Wallaby tour that I didn't think it was the right way to leave Union. In the end I'd virtually convinced myself to have one more season.

Before I'd left Britain I was approached by a Welsh selector on the night after the match against the Barbarians, our last game. He

The Switch

had asked me if I would come back the next season to play in a Barbarian side against Wales. I'd missed the experience of playing a Test at Cardiff Arms, the greatest Union stadium in the world; I'd played against Cardiff there, but it wasn't quite the same. Rugby Union is like a religion to the Welsh and when it is their country against another, the place is like magic.

It was a very appealing offer, but I told the guy I'd have to let him know. He told me it was an open invitation, and that the Welsh people would love to see more of me because they'd missed seeing me in the Test. It was a great honour and it made me start to wonder even more about what else I could achieve in the rah rah game.

The trip back was a fairly emotional one as could be expected with a bunch of close-knit sportsmen who had been away together for four months. There was a fair bit of talk about us sticking together and becoming a great Test side, and that we would say no to the offers to turn professional. It made it even harder to turn to League just then, but in the wash-up it didn't affect my thinking that much. I made my own decisions, and as it was it wasn't long before a few other 1975-76 Wallabies would turn pro—John Berne in 1976, John Ryan in 1977, Jim Hindmarsh in 1977, Ken Wright in 1979.

The second thoughts disappeared soon after my return. For starters, I had given a pretty young girl named Chris Minns an engagement ring before I'd left, and we arranged an engagement party shortly after I got back. We needed money to get married. Whitey had spoken to a few clubs and both Parramatta and Balmain were pretty keen to sign me. Dundas was in the Balmain junior area, but there wasn't a lot of doubt about where I would end up playing—back at Cumberland Oval.

I signed for $8000 a season, with a $6000 cash "backhander" thrown in. The cash "bonus" was a common under-the-lap payment at the time, which the Taxation Department eventually found out about in 1979 when they went through the books of Parramatta and other clubs in one of their periodic clampdowns. They got me, with the tax plus a penalty.

I had only wanted to sign for one year. I didn't know for sure if I'd be suited to League and wanted to play it by ear, but Parramatta wanted a three-year deal and I got talked around. They agreed to advance the money—a total of $24,000—to help Chris and I buy a house. The money was virtually a loan; the club charged me interest which was taken out of my match payments cheque each year.

So I had realised my dream of several years: to do well enough in Union to land a contract in League. I'd achieved far more than I thought I would in the amateur game. I didn't think at any stage I would win a Fairfax Cup, let alone as a 19-year-old. And I'd never expected to play for Australia; I had just wanted to play first grade. I hadn't set out to achieve anything in particular, but once I had reached those levels, the taste of success got to me.

I realised then that you should set yourself goals, to strive to achieve something. And this is a principle of life I've followed since—goal setting. I've set goals all the way during my League career and nine times out of 10 I've forced myself to achieve them through hard work, persistence and patience.

Rugby Union was good to me. I had a lot of good memories, a lot of terrific friends. I played with and against a lot of great players. I didn't have many heroes as such, but there were a few who stood out. Ken Catchpole, that little bloke I tried to belt in my first senior game, was one of the greatest halfbacks you could hope to see. John Hipwell was another I thought of as a legend. He was my Australian captain on the Wallaby tour and it was sad he didn't play more than two Tests on the '75 tour because of injury. Mark Loane was a great lock and a terrific bloke. He would have made it in League, too.

It's a difficult question to answer whether many of the top Union players would have done well in League, because dedication has a lot to do with success as does raw ability. Tony Shaw had the make-up to succeed. Gary Pearse had plenty of approaches, but I don't know if he would have been a success. Of the other guys who switched—Wright, Ryan, Hindmarsh and Berne—none represented at a high level nor fulfilled the expectations many had for them, although Berne did play a lot of first grade over several seasons.

I naturally had to inform the Parramatta Rugby Union Club of my intention to switch before the news came out in the papers. I called my coach Rod Phelps to tell him I had played my last game for him, and he was great. He'd expected it. But I couldn't say the same for my old club, which showed plenty of sour grapes. The committee took away my full membership of the club and informed me I could hold associate member rights only. I told them they could stick it. I've only been back to the Parramatta

The Switch

Union Club twice in the years since, and both times it was only to please a lot of friends who persuaded me. One was for a benefit for Martin Knight, the Parramatta centre who died tragically of leukaemia, and the other time was for a function I can't recall. It really annoyed me that the club could make such a big deal of me when I was its only international at the time, but once I had made the decision to try to earn some money out of the game, I was dropped like a hot spud.

The club wasn't alone in dropping me when I switched codes. My employers did the same. Alan Smith retrenched me only a few months into the 1976 season. The building game wasn't going that well and he reckoned he had to lay a couple of men off. I'd been there almost eight years and I wasn't far off getting long service leave. Despite being there a lot longer than quite a few others I got the chop. Smith said to me, "At least you've got your football money coming in." If only he knew how much I was getting.

Fortunately, Jack Argent, the Parramatta League treasurer, fitted me into his building company and I wasn't out of work for long. I stayed with Jack for a couple of years and I'll always be grateful.

Back in the workforce and a professional footballer, I took the plunge into matrimony on August 6, 1976. It was a Friday and we played North Sydney on the Sunday; there was no time for a honeymoon.

I had met Chris on a cruise back in January 1975—in the ship's sick bay. I was on holiday with 16 guys from Dundas Valley and Northmead. Chris was there with a girlfriend called Paula. I was on my way back to my cabin, rocking from side to side down the corridor, partly because of the very rough seas, possibly because I'd had a few beers. I saw Chris and Paula sitting in sick bay (for the same two reasons), so I wandered in and asked them if I could take them for a drink later. I certainly picked the right one out of the pair; as we were chatting that night Paula was sick all over a mate of mine.

We seemed to get on well from the start. Chris had long, straight blonde hair and was happy-go-lucky. We met on the second day of that cruise and ended up spending a lot of time together. When we got back to Sydney, Chris's mum was there to meet her as we got off the boat, but I thought I'd wait to make my big impression.

I gave Chris a call through the week, and arranged to go over to her place on the Saturday. (Actually, when we got off the boat she owed me $20, so she knew I'd come over.) I had no idea where Villawood was in Sydney's south-west. When I first heard that was where Chris lived, it sounded as if it was in Victoria or somewhere equally as foreign, but I hopped on my motorbike and went across to meet the parents. Apparently, Chris's mum hated anyone putting their feet on her lounge; I lobbed in, lit up a smoke, said how nice it was to meet her and then put my feet up. But she let me come again ... and, Chris still hasn't paid me back that $20.

I used to smoke a bit in those days, but within a couple of weeks of returning from the Wallaby tour I gave it up for good. Other than a big cigar I had after our first League grand final in 1976 which made me sick as a dog, I've only had the odd one over a beer—a handful in all these years.

When I got back from the Wallaby tour I hadn't played a lot of football and Parramatta had already been training for quite a few weeks. I went down to Cumberland for the first time on a Tuesday night, met coach Terry Fearnley who immediately impressed me, and hopped into the training, all keen to impress my new club. Compared to what I was used to in Union, it was a pretty heavy session and after a solid road run, I spewed my heart out. Right then and there I decided I was giving up the fags. I knew if I was going to make it I had to be fitter than the next bloke. And it didn't take me long to find out I had to be as tough as the next bloke as well.

Actually when I look back, 1976 was probably the most significant year of my life. It was the year I gave up smoking, the year I became a professional footballer, the year I was retrenched from my first job, the year we got married and the year we bought our first house.

Chris and I were married at St Marks Church, Granville, the same church in which her parents were wed. I remember the day well, and I also remember the minister, who was a Norths League fan and a Northern Suburbs Rugby Union supporter as well. He had red and black streamers on the door of the church to give us a bit of a stir. That was on a Friday, and Parramatta actually played Norths on the Sunday. I remember that too; my legs were pretty rubbery!

I had no bucks night and no honeymoon, football saw to that. We had a lot of family and friends at the wedding, but none of my League team-mates. There were quite a few from Union though, including Wallaby team-mates Jim Hindmarsh and Greg Cornelson.

The Switch

We were supposed to have been married in October, after the season ended, but the settlement on our house came through early so we made the wedding date in August and moved straight in to a nice three-bedroom brick home in Munro St, Greystanes, which we had bought for $42,000. We stayed there for three-and-a-half of our 11 years together. Now we are parents of two great kids, Benjamin and Kasey.

The 11 years haven't been all rosy though, mainly because of the pressures of football. It is not hard to see why so many marriages in Rugby League are not good ones and why so many don't last. At times I admit I became a stranger to my family because I was so preoccupied with my career—training, playing, attending promotions, touring sometimes for up to three months.

When I became a professional Rugby League player in February 1976 it changed our lives—in more ways than people realise.

Rugby League—The Beginning

THERE ARE A lot of my 280 Rugby League games for Parramatta that I just can't remember, but I certainly can't say that about my first. (Well, my first half game, anyway.) It was in reserve grade against Balmain at Cumberland Oval in the 1976 pre-season. It was the first game played under the new lights at Cumberland. One Tiger tried to turn the lights out, though, and those were mine.

It had been decided to give me a run in reserves to see how I went, and then bring me on in firsts if I handled things okay. The first time I took the ball up, Balmain's Neil (Bing) Pringle belted me with a beauty, as if to say "Welcome to Rugby League". He split my eye open and got penalised. It was probably the best way for me to start my new vocation. It got a good square-up later, and Pringle and I had a ding-dong battle in the first half before I was pulled off to be kept fresh for the first-grade Wills Cup game.

I probably owe Bing for that initiation. I learned from the outset you can't let anyone get on top of you; you give as much as you take, and I don't mean with fouls. At Parramatta, under all my coaches—Terry Fearnley, John Peard, Jack Gibson and John Monie—foul play was never tolerated, but you don't let the opposition intimidate you. I always played my football hard. I was a physical player. Sometimes I might have gone over the top, but in League you could soon sense who the soft players were. You soon smelled a weakness. It came under pressure. The good players could shine when the flow of the game was going their way, and the tough players would continue to shine and get stuck into the game when things weren't all their way.

That first night in a blue and gold jersey I came on in the last 20 minutes of first grade. We were beaten 6–5. I remember that too; my positional play let me down badly, I didn't know where I was supposed to be. Balmain scored a try in the corner to win the game and Mark Levy and I got the blame. It was my inexperience which caused the try. But I let a few Balmain players know I was around and I enjoyed the experience, though I didn't enjoy losing. I hated it, and I always have, no matter if it was a pre-season match, competition game, grand final or Test.

When I got to Parramatta I could tell that my sort of attitude hadn't been the norm. At the end of 1975 the Eels started to prove to themselves that winning was possible; with an incredible late run of wins under coach Norm Provan they had made a three-way play off for fifth spot with Wests and Balmain. They beat Balmain on Tuesday, Wests on Thursday and then knocked off Canterbury in the minor semi-final on the Sunday. When the 1976 season began the feeling was halfway between "well that was a fluke, I wonder how we'll go this year" and "winning is not bad, I want a feel of it again". Luckily Terry Fearnley had given Parramatta their second ever premiership title when he took the reserves to a grand-final victory in 1975 and was the right man to continue that success when he took over firsts in my first year.

As an observer from the Parramatta Union ranks in the five years before, the League club looked to be in a bit of a shemozzle. We had trained after the Leaguies on Tuesday and Thursday nights and obviously used to get there before they had finished. They always looked like a rag-tag group of people, players and officials. Really, it was like a bit of a bunfight. At that stage they were more often than not at the bottom of the ladder and seemed not to give two hoots. They were getting paid and having a good time off the field; that seemed good enough.

Parramatta's new era of success really began in '76, due mostly to the influence of Terry Fearnley and, I'd like to think, the injection of new players like John Peard, Mark Levy and myself.

On the field, things started to rev up and a new sort of belief in each other started to emerge. Off the field, the change was more gradual. Parramatta, like many clubs in the early and mid-1970s, was still administered by well-intentioned club stalwarts with chook-raffle type organisational skills. Secretary Bob Jones was a nice bloke, well-liked, who always said the right thing. He was too nice a bloke. I don't think he was the hardest worker or the smartest organiser around, and Fearnley did a lot of that side of things. President Stan Simpson was another really nice guy, but he was also part of the old-type regime who had led the club through a long, long stretch of lean times after four good years (1962–65) when the Eels made the semi-finals with some great players like Ken and Dick Thornett, Ron Lynch, Brian Hambly, Barry Rushworth, Billy Rayner and Bobby Bugden. Treasurer Jack Argent was the man who gave me a job after I was retrenched a few weeks into the season, for which I will always be grateful, but he was getting long in the tooth and like the other well-meaning hard triers, he had not kept pace with the new professionalism of the game.

In my 11 seasons with Parramatta the administration gradually moved with the times and became one of the most professional in the game, and that was largely due to the efforts of Denis Fitzgerald, a team-mate in my first few seasons. But, as many people knew, I didn't always see eye to eye with Fitzy or the club administration.

The knockers were at us all year in 1976. They reckoned we didn't have the guts or the talent to keep going through to the grand final. Funnily enough, deep down a lot of the team thought the same things, so it was a bit of a fairytale as things just kept unfolding until we were the first team to go into the grand final. From not believing we could even make it that far, we ended up knowing we could win the damn thing.

I had to get used to some big differences between Union and League in that first season. One of the hardest things I found in the first two months was the man-on-man, one-on-one situation in defence. I didn't mind it, but it just took some getting used to. In Union it was more a case of getting there and scuffling with a bloke until someone else came and joined the scuffle. In League it was important that you stopped the man ball and all. It was you against him, and gang tackles weren't the go then to the extent they are now. For those first couple of months, the insides of my arms, right up to my shoulders, were permanently bruised because of all the tackling. I just wasn't used to that amount of tackling in Rugby Union.

The positional play was the other big difference. Luckily I was helped a lot by my team-mates, who used to talk to me and tell me where to fill in. And Terry Fearnley made it easier by giving me a bit of a free rein; he didn't say, "I want you to do this and you should be doing that". In many ways I played League the same as I played Union. I just tried to be as close to the ball as possible and whenever "they" had the ball, I moved in for the kill.

I started my League days in the second-row, and hated it. I hated the way you packed into scrums; you had to be a contortionist to

I would never have made it in Australian Rules on the strength of this grab for the ball in a match against Manly. But, as always, I gave it a go.

Terry Fearnley was my first coach at Parramatta Rugby League Club. He was a quiet, well-respected man who deserved a premiership medal.

put your head up the front-rower's bum, hug onto the other second-rower, and give the hooker a shove. I don't think Ray Higgs liked it much either. I reckon we were the fastest breaking second-rowers in the history of the game. The less time we spent in the scrums, the better.

Unfortunately I had to stay in the second-row for a good part of that first season, but other than in the scrums, I always played the game then just the same as I did when I became a lock. And I can be thankful that I had pretty much of a dream run in my first year in the professional game.

I struck up a combination straight away with John Peard. I scored 12 tries in my first season, seven in my first six premiership games, and most of them came from chasing Peardy's bombs. It didn't take me long to realise Peardy had the best kicking game in the competition. It was like he could put the ball on a string. Fearnley decided to try a revolutionary form of attack: to kick the ball high into the in-goal so that the defending fullback would be tackled and we'd regain possession. A kick is only as good as the chasers, I had decided, so every time Peard put it up, I'd try to be the first one there. It started to spread like a disease through the team; the other players started to realise that if Peard could pinpoint the ball so well we were going to put a lot of pressure on teams and we might pick up a few tries for ourselves. Nothing motivates a player more than the chance to have "try" against his name in the scoreline.

Peardy and I didn't rehearse the kick and chase. It came naturally. I used to chase the high ball and I had so much confidence in Peardy putting them on the spot that I didn't look up until I got there. I'd run straight for the spot where the fullback or whoever had planted themselves to take the ball and just as I got there I'd look for the ball. Nine times out of 10 it was right where it was supposed to be so it was simply a matter of outjumping the opposition. Being on the run while the defenders were standing still, the jump wasn't that hard.

John Peard had a lot to do with the revival of Parramatta. He was more than just "The Bomber". Peardy was a very, very good low tackler, he had great hands, could read a game pretty well and, in 1976, before Mick Cronin arrived, proved to be a pretty reliable goalkicker. He was a thorough professional in his approach to the game, his treatment of injuries and in his attitude to training, and a lot of that rubbed off.

Ray Higgs also had a major influence on Parramatta's new fortunes. Higgsy was a straight bloke. Fearnley picked him as captain and, outside the club at least, it was regarded as pretty much a shock. He'd been there in 1975 and had been seen as a bit of a hot-head. He was hard and ruthless and he led by example. He didn't have a lot of skills, but he was a very hard defensive player. In fact, I rate him and John Baker, neither of them big men, as the best defensive players I played with—they left some people laying around the ground.

Higgsy could tell at first meeting whether you were weak in your make-up or not. He called a spade a spade and could get pretty abusive when he wanted to. If you weren't strong right back to him, he could sense a weakness right away. Mark Levy was never impressed with Higgsy; Ray always gave him a hard time. And it was the same with Geoff Gerard; he and Levy never knew quite where they stood with Higgsy. I didn't mind him. If he called you an imbecile or whatever, and you stood right up to him, he'd admire you. I always thought I got on pretty well with him. He didn't mind hard tactics and he seemed to get the best out of people in a completely different way than Terry Fearnley did.

Terry was a quiet bloke and a very intelligent person. He never yelled, nor swore. He knew how to get the best out of his players and how to give them confidence, and that wasn't by ranting and raving. If you did something wrong, it was pointed out to you fairly, but he would never embarrass a player in front of his team-mates.

I always felt for Terry because he never got that premiership he had chased with such genuine ambition. Maybe he lacked that little bit of "kill" in his coaching or his attitude. Maybe he didn't quite have that edge that Jack Gibson was able to give us a few years later. But I will always regard him as a very good coach, and as a very big reason why Parramatta are a success these days. And he's also a very good friend.

He was ready to give coaching away in 1975 when he was beaten by Paul Broughton in a ballot for the first-grade spot at Balmain. Terry had played with Jack Gibson for many years at Easts, and then became understudy coach to him, firstly at Newtown and then as reserve-grade coach when Gibbo's Roosters won the 1974 competition. Norm Provan asked him to be his understudy at Parramatta after hearing he'd missed the Balmain job. Terry reckoned his friends told him he was mad because Parramatta were such a lowly club at the time, but it ended up being the best move he ever made.

He had five years at Parramatta, four as top-grade coach, and every team he had made the semi-finals. He took a few years off before having a season at Wests; the Magpies were having a rough trot but Terry took them to the semis against all the odds. Then he had two seasons at Cronulla, his local team (he lived at Yowie Bay), but didn't have a lot of success. He finished his coaching days by taking NSW to its first ever win in a State of Origin series in 1985, and coaching Australia in that same year. It was his second time as national coach, having had the 1977 Australian World Cup side while at Parra.

The bespectacled Fearnley had the respect of everyone at Parramatta and it was only through his persistence that John Peard and Michael Cronin played for the club. He wouldn't give up until he got them. And he went so close to bringing off a historic double: Parramatta's first ever first-grade premiership and a premiership for a coach in his debut first-grade season. It would have been fantastic for Terry to have come to the club and given us a reserve-grade grand-final win then a first-grade grand-final win in his first two seasons.

I remember well the night after that first grand final in '76. We were pretty down after losing and we all went back to the Leagues club to drown our sorrows. Terry was a little late arriving and he explained later in a book on the Parramatta Club's history *Quest for Glory*, that he went home first and was so dejected he didn't want to go to the club to face the people. But his wife Betty convinced him he should.

When he got there the Parramatta fans treated him like a hero. They were patting him on the back and thanking him for the club's greatest year. His face just lit up, he couldn't believe it. I'll always regard Terry Fearnley as a hero too but, unfortunately, he went down in the record books as an unsung hero. Jack Gibson and John Monie were recorded as first-grade winning coaches and so was John Peard, who won a Tooth Cup in 1980. Terry took us so close but didn't get a trophy in first grade like the others.

September Sadness

I BLAME TWO people and two things for Parramatta not winning its first ever first-grade grand final in 1976. Firstly, skipper Ray Higgs and kicker John Peard, for some reason, refused to use our kicking game to kick us out of danger from our own quarter; and secondly, Parramatta had played their own "grand final" two days before the real thing.

That happened to be an incredible parade by the players through the city of Parramatta on the Thursday night before the grand final. I couldn't believe the timing of it. I'm not saying it was not a good idea; Parramatta had for a long time been the easybeats of the Sydney competition and in 1976 we suddenly became the pride of the west. Win or lose on grand-final day, the people of the area would still see us as their heroes. The parade was fine but it should have gone ahead after the game.

You don't do such a thing the Thursday night before a Saturday grand final. Not only did it drain most of the players, it brought them to a high too early. You wouldn't give a champion two-year-old a full-scale gallop two days before the Golden Slipper because you would flatten it for the big race, but by parading the Parramatta team before an absolutely massive crowd on that Thursday night, that's what happened to the Eels—they were flattened. Halfway through the grand final against Manly you could tell quite a few of us were drained. I don't know whose idea it was to put on that parade, but it was one of the biggest mistakes Parramatta have made. And I have noticed it has never happened again.

It was an incredible experience. We hopped on to a float at Cumberland Oval and headed down to the main street, Church Street, then along to Westfield Shoppingtown at the other end of Parramatta. There were an estimated 60,000 to 70,000 people lining the streets. It was amazing. There were people hanging off the overhead railway bridge and when we got inside Westfield it was mayhem. We couldn't get through the crowd to the stage and the place was vibrating at the foundations.

While there was an electric atmosphere that night, I was worried all along what it would do to our build-up. We had a fairly young side with only John Peard having played in a grand final before. I was only 23 and in my first season of League, but compared to most of the team I had had much more big game experience with two Union grand finals and seven Tests. I knew how draining the build-up to a grand final could be.

On match day the atmosphere was incredible again. There was a crowd of 57,343 and it was the first of the recent grand-final days when a big bill of entertainment was put on with dancing girls, skydivers, and balloons everywhere. As well there was a giant mechanical eel which did a circuit of the ground. The place was just buzzing; I've probably never felt as nervous before a match. The atmosphere just came down and touched us as we walked from the dressing room in the members stand down through the gate which so many great footballers and cricketers had passed, then onto the field.

Once the ball was kicked-off I just put everything but football out of my mind. That is one thing I've always been able to do: shut everything out once the football began. Jim Porter scored after only 11 minutes, from a John Peard bomb. Peardy converted and we led 5–0. A try by Phil Lowe and a couple of goals put Manly in front 7–5 just before the break. Then Peardy levelled the scores with a penalty from an incident in which Terry Randall flattened Ray Higgs with a right hook that broke Higgsy's jaw. He showed plenty of courage to play on.

In the second half Manly kept us pinned down in our own territory, and then referee Gary Cook took offence to how John Kolc was feeding our scrum; two scrum penalties put Manly ahead. Most people blame Neville Glover and probably the most infamous dropped pass in grand-final history for us losing that game, but I don't agree. That pass came down the right flank with 12 minutes to go. Big centre John (Lazy) Moran broke a tackle and, I thought, was going to force his way over himself. But about 10 metres out, the pass, which wasn't a great one from Moran, went right through Glover's hands and into touch—with the line open. To be honest, as I ran over to pack into the scrum I still thought we were going to win. I never thought of it as the match-winning try gone begging.

What I found hard to accept was that until that point, we had spent most of the second half trying to run the ball out of our own quarter or waiting until the last tackle to kick. I don't know why Higgsy as skipper and Peardy as our tactical kicker didn't just reef the ball downfield on the second or third tackle to take the pressure off us. That's why we lost the game on four goals from scrum penalties. We were feeding too many scrums close to our own line.

As it was we scored the only try of the second half, by Geoff Gerard, and all up scored two tries to one. Most people at the ground claimed we were the better side, but Manly had the right tactics. They tried to play the game in our territory and sweated on our mistakes. And it worked. Had we played the game in their territory and just tackled, which was the thing we did best, it would have been a different story.

Things were getting desperate late in the game and we almost pulled off a miraculous win with the famous "wedge", an ingenious move I had brought over from Rugby Union. I had raised it in discussion a couple of weeks before the grand final and we practised it while in camp at Narrabri the weekend before the grand final. Manly were the minor premiers, but after we beat St George 31-6 in the preliminary semi-final and then dispatched Manly for the third time that season in the major semi (23-17), we went into the grand final first and earned a weekend's rest. Terry Fearnley thought it was a good idea to take us away from the hype and go bush, and while we were there we started to rehearse the unusual move which we thought might just come in handy.

It involved us forming a wedge formation, virtually the same as a scrum but in reverse, with one player at the front of an arrow formation carrying the ball. I think the person who devised it in Union was Darryl Haberecht, the Country coach who was also responsible for the ball-up-the-jumper trick. Before it could work we needed a volunteer who would run the risk of being used as the "tip" of the wedge. I mentioned that it happened to be a very good chance of creating a try, and as soon as that three-letter word was mentioned our lanky hooker Ron Hilditch's ears pricked and his hand went up to volunteer. Ace Hilditch didn't score a lot of tries and he immediately saw this as his big chance.

It must have been inside the final five minutes when we got a

September Sadness

penalty that brought us about 15 metres out from Manly's line. We took up our positions, Hilditch got the ball and the wedge charged for Manly's line. The only way to stop it was to tackle the ball carrier, ball-and-all, and had Graham Eadie not woken up to that and wrapped his big frame around Hilditch, we would have scored for sure. Eadie, one of the strongest front-on tacklers in the game, brought the wedge to a halt about a metre from the tryline. When the full-time hooter went it was 13–10. Parramatta had failed.

Another thing I remember about that grand final was Terry Randall hitting me with one of the best tackles I have ever copped. I was running down the sideline and Randall came across in cover. He got his timing absolutely perfect and just about snapped me in two. He put me well over the touchline and for a second or two I really thought about getting back up. I pushed myself off the turf and went into the scrum, but when I say I went into the scrum, it was really a case of just leaning on it.

For the third straight year my team had gone down in a grand final, and I didn't like it one bit. I started to wonder whether I would ever know what it would be like to do a victory lap.

One season later, in 1977, Parramatta came in minor premiers by a mile. We were clearly the best team all season. We had brought Mick Cronin from the bush and he was just what we needed. He came with a big reputation as a goalkicker who had already recorded a heap of incredible point-scoring feats for Australia since his shock selection in the 1973 Kangaroos. Ironically, against St George in his first Sydney grand final, he missed a goal right near fulltime that he rued for the rest of his career.

Parramatta was feeling pretty good going into the grand final against St George, who were a very young side called "Bath's Babes", their coach being Harry Bath. We had won the minor premiership, and the club championship for the second year, Mick Cronin had scored a club record of 225 points in his first season and he also received the Rothmans Medal (which he won again the following season). We had gone down 10–5 to Saints in the semi-final, and for the first time we hadn't gone straight into the grand final. We had to play Easts in the final.

We had really began to rely on John Peard's bombs and looking back now it was amazing how we'd got away with it for so long. (I suppose it revolutionised the game—to the extent where the League brought in a rule to stamp it out in 1985.) In that semi-final against St George, the Dragons started firing their nippy little

Pound for pound, kilo for kilo, Johnny Kolc (left) and John Baker were two of the toughest players I teamed up with in either League or Union.

halfback Mark Shulman to out from the second-marker position to put pressure on Peardy. They had their wingers drop back to support their fullback, and they also had a five-eighth, Rod McGregor, who was one of the best low tacklers I've come across. He didn't last on the scene very long, although he played for NSW, but what he did do was shatter the confidence of our most consistent forward for so many seasons, Denis Fitzgerald. Fitzy was very tall and lean, and his main method of beating a tackle was with the fend. But McGregor cut him down, tackling too low for the fend almost everytime Fitzy ran.

When it came to the grand final, Fearnley decided to start with John Baker in the front-row and put Fitzy on the bench. McGregor had a blinder in defence. The game was really tight and with minutes remaining the only try had been scored by St George fullback Ted Goodwin when he chipped and regathered in the in-goal. With a minute to go we were behind 9-6. Then we got into the St George quarter and Cronin put me into a narrow gap. I got to about five metres from the line and as I was about to go into touch I sensed someone looming in support just to my left. I got the ball over my shoulder and centre Ed Sulkowicz stepped around the Saints' fullback and scored. It was 9-all and we had the best goalkicker in the competition to line up the conversion about seven metres inside the right touchline.

As we walked back to halfway no one thought that Crow was going to miss the goal. No one at all. We all thought we were going to win the grand final. I was in shock when the ball went to the right. We had to go to extra time.

After 10 minutes each way it was still 9-all. At that point we should have turned around and played another five minutes each way or been declared joint premiers. People had come that day, and so had the players, to see the championship decided, but the NSW Rugby League had no rule in their books to cover such an event, so the greedy bastards decided to bring us all back the following weekend to go through it all again. I have always felt that greed was the NSWRL's main motivation for a replay; it wanted another chance to have a big crowd and a big gate at the SCG. The game, however, became the greatest anti-climax in Rugby League history.

Parramatta were never a chance in the replay, a game I have very scant recollections of and have never seen on video. The reason I can't remember much is that I had the you-know-what belted out of me by St George's Rod Reddy, who, with an apparent licence to kill, received five cautions from referee Gary Cook in the first half, all for fouls on me. And Reddy still stayed on the field! Although I can't remember much, from what I've been told, he belted me from pillar to post. And I finished the game with teeth marks on my forehead, courtesy of a Saints player.

The fact that a player could get four more cautions after laying me out the first time we had come into contact must cast doubts upon the referee's performance. Cook looked under pressure during the first grand final and, according to other Parramatta players, looked under more strain the second time. He retired two seasons later.

Parramatta was flat during the second game. St George had the advantage from the time the full-time hooter finally had gone the Saturday before. For starters, its young players were always regarded as the underdogs and responded well to Harry Bath's coaching. We had a heap of older players like Jim Porter, John Peard, John Baker, Ray Higgs and Graham Olling. I think Saints had seven players aged 21 or less.

And we took injuries into the game. Both Graham Olling and John Baker had broken hands and shouldn't have played, but Terry Fearnley obviously didn't want to break up the combination we'd had all season and thought it would inspire us by having them there, since we'd been through it together all season. I thought it was suicide. You can't take players into the big games unless they are fit.

Another thing that distracted us was Ed Sulkowicz's wedding the night before the replay. He had planned it for a week after the grand final and there was no way he could put it off. Most of the team attended. It was hard to get motivated for the coming game, that was for sure. It was a non-event. The grand final had been the week before, not this week.

Saints belted us. I vaguely remember at half-time I was in no-man's-land. I didn't know where I was. Fearnley came up to me and told me he was going to take me off. I felt as though I hadn't even played. "No, I feel okay now," I told him. "I'm great, I'm right to go back out." I can't remember a thing after that.

There has been a lot of discussion about what else had happened at half-time. Supposedly there was a blow up between Ray Higgs and Fearnley about our failure to retaliate, and although I can't say because my mind was pretty blank at the time, what

Ray Higgs on the boil. I wish he had shown the same head of steam in the first ever first-grade grand final replay in 1977.

I will say is that when I was getting bashed around in the first half, I didn't get much support from my skipper Ray Higgs. When I was captain in later years and one of my players was getting some unfair attention, I'd go to his aid or square up a bit later. I always thought of it as my duty. I didn't get any support that day. So, too those stories that say Higgsy wanted to retaliate but Fearnley wouldn't let him, all I can say is I wish Higgsy had showed a bit more fire than he did.

Apparently there had been plenty of drama between Higgs and Fearnley off the field leading into that grand final. I was oblivious to it all and it certainly didn't upset the team on the field or at training, but it was becoming obvious there was some tension between the two. Only a few weeks after the grand-final replay Higgsy left to play for Manly, even though there was a year remaining on his contract. It was all over the blow-up with Fearnley.

The story came out that Fearnley had wanted Bob O'Reilly to return to the club (he had left for Penrith after the 1975 season), but Higgsy wouldn't have a bar of it. That caused all sorts of fireworks. Apparently it ended in a shouting match in Bob Jones's office and one of the pair had to go. Higgs left and Parramatta missed out on O'Reilly as well, who went to Easts.

I think the captaincy became too much for Ray Higgs, although I still regard him as one of the most fearless players and captains I have played with. He was certainly a bit of a strange person, and I think he just became a little greedy at the end. He wanted this and that and Terry wouldn't give in to him. I suppose it must have been similar to the situation between Steve Mortimer and Warren Ryan at Canterbury in the mid-1980s.

When a rift between a captain and coach develops, the only satisfactory way out is for one of them to leave. Canterbury wouldn't let Mortimer go when he finally requested it and it was incredible that the Bulldogs were still able to be such a threat in the competition with Mortimer and Ryan both there and not getting on. I know if I had ever been at loggerheads with my coach while I was at Parramatta it would have been intolerable. I would have stood down as captain or left. Fortunately John Monie and I, and Terry Fearnley and I when I was captain in 1978 and '79 (I succeeded Higgs) had no such problems ... although I stood down in 1980 and years later, under Monie, I was asked to concede the captaincy to Peter Sterling.

The Hartley Feud

THE YEARS 1978 and 1979 were very significant in my career. In '78 I became the Parramatta captain, and first played League for Australia, then, in 1979, I won the Rothman's Medal, the Harry Sunderland Medal and a whole heap of awards.

Both seasons, however, were soured by the fact that I was sent off in my last match of each year, both times by referee Greg Hartley.

The name Hartley doesn't go down well with people at Parramatta, and least of all me. The feeling began to surface towards the end of the 1978 season when his elevation from reserve-grade to grand-final referee was seen by many as a great surprise.

With six rounds remaining Hartley was in reserve grade. He went on to control the grand final (and replay) despite a wave of objection from many people, and several clubs, including Parramatta.

I certainly couldn't come to grips with Hartley's flamboyant and unpredictable style of refereeing that season, but the team that eventually put us out of the premiership and won the competition, Manly, somehow could. They had plenty of practice of course; after Hartley's elevation they had him in eight of their remaining 11 matches. They seemed to "adapt" to Hartley's style where some other teams couldn't.

In our semi-final against Manly, we were belted from pillar to post, but Hartley just let it go on. We led Manly 13-3, and after Hartley caned us 7-1 in the second-half penalties we drew 13-all.

We had to play a replay on the Wednesday, and unfortunately, our reserve grade had to play a replay of their semi-final as well, so our stocks were pretty depleted. Graham Murray, Greg Heddles and Bob Jay were all ruled out with head injuries suffered in questionable tackles. Our fullbacks Mark Levy and Phil Mann were also out, which meant a kid called Peter Sterling was called up to make his first-grade debut.

We went down to Manly 17–11, and again Hartley was referee. It has been well documented since that Manly's try which clinched the match for them was scored by Steve Martin, on the seventh tackle. It was the third time in that game that Manly was given seven tackles instead of six. Three times Parramatta were allowed only five tackles.

That wasn't the only time it's been found referees erred in counting tackles, and I've always maintained they need help in that area because it is so easy to miscount when under pressure. But the fact remains on that day it proved very costly for Parramatta.

Since that week in 1978, Greg Hartley became a dirty word at Parramatta. I had regarded him as just about the best referee I had played under—until then. He had always been a show-pony, but he kept up with the play, positioned himself well, and seemed to understand things about the game that other referees didn't.

But his promotion from reserve grade to the number-one rated ref controlling the grand final in only a matter of weeks, and then going on the Kangaroo tour, dismayed a number of people.

One possible explanation was that the referees' ranks were split into two distinct factions, and had been for years. One group appeared anti-Hartley while another was pro-Hartley, and in the end it was obvious which faction won out. The bottom line was that he was publicly proved to have made several glaring errors in his refereeing, yet Hartley kept the number-one rating.

Parramatta wasn't the only club to protest against Hartley in those days. Wests coach Roy Masters also made his feelings known during the 1978 final series and publicly stated he didn't want Hartley as referee. The feud spread to five clubs with their coaches Terry Fearnley (Parramatta), Masters, Jack Gibson (Souths), Norm Provan (Cronulla) and Arthur Beetson (Easts) all claiming they had no confidence in Hartley. Yet, under all the public dissatisfaction and proof of the errors he'd made, the people in power persisted in giving him the top games right through to the grand-final replay.

Eight Manly players went on the 1978 Kangaroo tour, the benefit of being premiers, I suppose, but one player didn't go. John Harvey decided to pass-up selection and stay home. The next year Harvey transferred to Eastern Suburbs, a move which signalled a sudden downturn in his career.

The Hartley Feud

Many people, and not just those from Parramatta, reckoned Harvey raised his elbows dangerously when he ran. Great attention was brought to it while he was at Manly, but he was allowed to get away with it. The next season, when Harvey was at Easts, he was sent off early in the season, in the first minute of the game against his old club Manly—for using his elbow. The referee? Hartley.

I could never figure it out, nor could plenty of my team-mates. One season Harvey could get away with his questionable style, then another year and another club, he was sent off. Harvey was never the same player after that and didn't last in first grade for too many more years.

Greg Hartley was too flashy, too daring and he had a big head. I had the impression he felt he was the centre of attraction at a football game, not the players. He loved to see his name in print, and if possible the headlines. It didn't matter if it was good press or bad press.

In a couple of games in which I played under him he bawled players out, or asked me as captain to tell such and such to cut it out because "he's ruining my game". It was as if he was the main attraction and the players were the support artists.

He belittled players with his manner of speaking down to them. A lot of players hated him for that. One day at Brookvale Oval, when Arthur Beetson was playing for Parramatta (I was injured at the time and sitting in the players' area near the sideline), Hartley chastised Beetson so spitefully that you could hear his remarks from the sideline. Arthur Beetson was a legend, probably the greatest ball-playing forward ever to lace a boot, and was near the end of his illustrious career. Hartley spoke to him as if Beetson was a schoolboy.

In the final series of 1978, Manly intentionally intimidated their opponents and were never pulled up for it—except on one occasion when John Gray was sent off. Then, in the semi-final replay, I was sent off for punching an opponent, Graham Eadie, on the ground. Hartley obviously missed the "incident"; all he saw was Eadie on the ground bleeding from the head and me scuffling with a couple of Manly players. Off I went. And away went our chances of winning the match.

The next Monday night I was exonerated when it was found I hadn't touched Eadie. There was not one scrap of evidence to back up the charge. He had accidentally copped a boot.

Considering that, plus the many other errors Hartley was found

Greg Hartley in his typically theatrical fashion, has a few words of wisdom to me. He had a few run-ins with Parramatta by the end of the 1970s.

Referees have never been my favourite people, but their task is thankless, and is made more difficult by the pace of today's game and the advent of television replays. Above: Barry Barnes makes his point. Below: John Gocher gives me 10 minutes in the sin-bin at the SCG.

to have made, I always wondered how he kept the number-one rating right through to the grand final. Parramatta complained, but to no avail. In the next few years we complained every time we thought we had a right to. Most times it was against Hartley. We got nowhere and each time Manly had a go at us, branding us whingers.

Parramatta made their hate for Hartley public. We didn't hide it. At the height of the war, Hartley was kept away from Parramatta and we went for almost a full season without having him at Cumberland Oval. The way we highlighted his mistakes had a lot to do with that, just as it seemed to do in later years when clubs complained about referees. During 1986 and 1987 it was no coincidence that Canterbury rarely got Kevin Roberts, Souths and Manly seemed to be kept at a distance from Bill Harrigan after some controversial run-ins, and the appointments boys seemed to avoid mixing Parramatta with Mick Stone.

There was no love lost between Parramatta and Hartley for a number of years, but it was ironic that he was at centre stage when we broke the premiership drought by beating Newtown in the 1981 grand final. It was even more ironic that it was his last match before he retired. But we got no sweetheart deals from Hartley that day, I assure you.

After being sent off in Parramatta's last match in 1978, I wouldn't have dreamt it could happen again the next year. In '79, in the final we lost to Canterbury, Hartley was referee again. But this time I can't blame him for my dismissal. He acted on a touch judge's report, the linesman graphically describing how I had done everything but bring out a meat cleaver to Canterbury's Chris Mortimer. Hartley had no choice but to dismiss me.

We had kicked off with a high, shallow kick and I charged through after it. I didn't take my eyes off the ball once, and as Mortimer waited for it, I skittled him unintentionally. I was charged with striking a player not in possession of the ball.

That day strengthened my dislike of linesmen, who are a hindrance more than a help to referees because of the untimely way they run on to the field, as if they are leading the cavalry. And usually it's to report something that happened right under the referee's nose.

There was one flag-waver I hated as much as he obviously hated me—Barry Wiseman. He wasn't the one responsible for me being sent off that day against Canterbury, nor the time a year before,

The Hartley Feud

but he was the man responsible when I was sent off in 1984 for the third and last time in my 11 seasons in League. The charge was tripping. It was a Cumberland throw that had gone wrong, but to this day I maintain I grabbed the player, Royce Ayliffe, with my hands first, which, under the laws of the game, meant it was not a trip. And I also maintained that the freeze-frame video evidence in Jim Coman's judiciary show didn't clearly prove it had been a trip.

The point was that Wiseman ran from the far touchline to report me for something that happened no more than 15 metres away from the other touchline. He must have eaten a lot of carrots because he saw something the other touch judge and the referee missed. From that day, almost every time Wiseman had a Parramatta game he reported me for something. And normally it wasn't just once a game, but more likely two, three or four times. He was typical of most touch judges; if it was a television match they would make an extra special effort to get on to the field and in front of the cameras.

My lack of respect for touch judges went on to make history. I became the first player—or member of any club—to be fined for comments over referees or touch judges. It was in 1984. The NSW Rugby League had brought in a rule forbidding public criticism of this protected species by players, coaches or officials of a club. Anyone who broke the commandment was automatically fined $1000.

That law had been in operation for a season and a bit and, despite plenty of fairly direct flouting of the rule, and several veiled comments which left little to the imagination, no one had been fined. I thought I would take the odds and speak my mind on touch judges in my *Rugby League Week* column. I simply said they were inconsistent in the way they decided to come off their line and report incidents. They were ignoring back play and stifling the game by running right across field to report things that happened right in front of the referee.

What sparked my comments was a reserve-grade game the previous Sunday between Parramatta and South Sydney. A Souths player came in and belted my brother Donald, who was playing for Parramatta. It happened not more than five metres in front of the touch judge, but he looked the other way as if to suggest he hadn't seen it. Donald is very unlike me. He is not an aggressive person and certainly not an aggressive player. You could belt him in the mouth and he wouldn't retaliate; he would more likely apologise for having his face in the way. Not long after getting belted, Donald got whacked again. This time it really hurt him and he hit the deck and stayed down injured. Again it happened right near the same touch judge, but again he looked the other way as if he hadn't seen it. It made me boil. That night when I was doing my RLW column, I got rid of my anger.

By the end of that week Parramatta had been fined. Under the rules, the player's club was asked to show reason why it should not be fined for the player's action. Before I knew what had happened Parramatta secretary Denis Fitzgerald decided the club did not have any reason to suggest why it shouldn't be fined—before I'd had a chance to talk to him or defend myself. Fitzy was a member of the NSWRL board then, and I was upset that he didn't give me any chance to defend the case. I was ruled guilty before even going into court. The club passed the $1000 fine on to me, but *Rugby League Week*, unhappy that comments by other people, particularly coaches, had gone unpunished, volunteered to pay the fine for me.

Although referees have not been my favourite people, I certainly don't envy their task. It is a very difficult and thankless job, and generally they try hard. And they are human; they make errors just like players. All I've ever asked from them was consistency, yet that is the main thing they lack.

They have probably picked up their game in most areas in the past few years except consistency. Referees generally are fitter and faster (because they have to be), but I don't think that they are any smarter.

As the game has become faster and the video age has put refs under so much more pressure, one referee is not enough on the football field anymore. He needs help with either in-goal adjudications or a second referee on the field of play. I haven't got the answers about such a system working, whether each referee gets half the field each, or one watches the attacking team while the other watches the defending team, but the two-referee system is worth a chance. And more than the chance it was given during the pre-season of 1987. The system was trialled in a couple of games but seemed to be put back on the League's "too-hard" shelf and never mentioned again. I don't even know what conclusions the League made from the trial run because, to my knowledge, its ideas on the matter never left its Phillip Street headquarters.

The Hartley Feud

In many cases referees don't help themselves. Too many of them in recent years have tried to copy Hartley's tough-man, "I'm-the-boss" attitude. They have built a barrier between themselves and the players. They talk down to the players. They try to be dictators. Still, my main beef is that they are not consistent. I would rather have a referee who was consistently bad, as long as it was for both teams.

The greatest mystery of the modern game is how a team can be penalised and penalised and penalised one week, then become angels the next. Or vice versa. Football teams just don't work like that. They don't lose or gain discipline in a week. It all has to do with a referee's pet hate, or the League's well publicised clampdowns on specific areas of the game, none of which were ever maintained for more than a few weeks. Or it is simply a referee's own inconsistent interpretations.

My opinions on a few of the referees I had the good fortune—or misfortune— to play under during my career in many ways outline their standing within the game.

Kevin Roberts: Sometimes "Bilko" was quite good, sometimes he was bad. I'm glad I'm not a policeman (like Detective Sergeant Roberts) because St George's Craig Young was and Roberts gave him a hell of a time on the football field. On his day Roberts was as good as any referee in the modern era—he had control. He stayed in the game two seasons too long after refereeing the 1985 grand final.

John Gocher: He looked like being a great referee, but became too much like Hartley—a show-pony. Towards the end of his career he became a very shaky referee. He could not handle explosive situations, lost confidence as well as his nerve. In the end he stayed in reserve grade, but the League convinced him he was better off giving it away and not stand in the way of younger blokes.

Giles O'Donnell: Like Greg Hartley, he was a short guy and took it out on anyone taller than him, which was usually everyone including the halfbacks. Any dicey situation got out of hand with him in charge, and I really think his height was a drawback; he had trouble seeing over the players.

Bill Harrigan: This young bloke has the makings of an excellent referee. He is fit, keeps up with the play, and is keen to do well, but he was thrown to the wolves in his first season of first grade in 1986. He was given a couple of television games and Monday night games, and he just wasn't ready for that sort of pressure.

Then his ego seemed to run away with him. He wanted to prove how tough he was with the players, spoke far too harshly to them, and became unapproachable even for team captains.

Barry Barnes: I wouldn't have him refereeing in under-23s, let alone first grade. He's inconsistent, lacks authority, and seems to have an uncontrollable fetish for running 20 metres across field in the opening couple of minutes of the game to penalise a team for offside.

Eddie Ward: This bloke is a great referee. I've always had a lot of time for him, and it is a great pity he fell out of favour with the men who control the game in Queensland, particularly Ron McAuliffe. Everytime he refereed an interstate match or Wednesday night cup game at Lang Park, he gave both sides a fair go, which is something I wouldn't say for another Queenslander, Barry Gomersall.

Barry Gomersall: His nickname is "Grasshopper", but that was about the nicest thing anyone from NSW ever called him. Despite Eddie Ward being twice the referee, every time we went to Lang Park in the 1980s Gomersall was at the helm. All I can say is that I could never follow any of his rulings and, for my liking, he was far too inconsistent.

Julien Rascagneres: He was a very fair referee. He made mistakes and at times he was hard to follow, but it was the same for both sides. And he always tried to let a game flow. The first time I met him, when he came to Australia in 1983, I got on exceptionally well with the Frenchman. He couldn't speak English and I couldn't speak French, so we needed an interpreter to communicate, but I sat down and spoke with him for hours. A lovely person.

English referees: I don't want to talk about them. I haven't found a good one yet.

Ray Shrimpton: He was the New Zealander sent over to be a neutral referee in the first two Tests against Great Britain at the Sydney Cricket Ground in 1984. His performance then rates with the worst I have witnessed. He was forever behind the play, some of his decisions completely baffled the players, and he had no idea how to control foul play. I think they were the only Test matches he ever refereed, thank heavens.

I don't dislike all referees, and I have found a couple I don't mind. There were plenty of games in which I thought the referee was good, but I can't remember them exactly. That's the way it should be, because if you can't remember the referee it means he did the job he was supposed to, he was inconspicuous, and he wasn't noticed amongst all the great football. The focus, as it always should be, was on the players.

The 14th Kangaroos

FRANK STANTON has to take a lot of credit for the success of the 1978 and '82 Kangaroos. With so many great players in those sides, probably anyone could have coached us to victory when it came to on-field tactics; we didn't need any revolutionary moves, and we were a class above the Poms by then in speed, strength and fitness. But the biggest danger on the tour was to let it become a social outing like at least one English side had treated its trip to Australia. Frank Stanton proved a master at keeping us fit, united and hungry.

Plenty of Test players who came under him reckoned he did it in an impersonal way and in many ways he could be vindictive, but as long as you trained hard, played hard and did the right thing under his many rules, he was all right.

He became Test coach at the same time I became a Test player. He retired as Test coach the same time I retired as a Test player. In my 22 Tests for Australia, Stanton was coach for 20 of them. We saw a lot of each other through football, but we would never regard ourselves as great friends. Nor enemies. We were just player and coach.

It was pretty obvious why Frank Stanton was called "Cranky Franky". On the 1978 Kangaroo tour he was like an old-fashioned English schoolmaster. He ruled with an iron fist. I didn't mind so much, but plenty of my team-mates did. Stanton's other common nickname was "Biscuits", which he had acquired as a red-headed halfback on the 1963 Kangaroo tour because of his ginger "nuts". But Biscuits and Cranky were about the best names he ever got. A lot of players called him a whole lot worse, particularly on that '78 tour.

Frank Stanton was a hard man, a disciplinarian. When we went on a Kangaroo tour for three months he didn't want us slackening, which could be easy to do when 28 players get together overseas. He kept us on our toes and he didn't try to gain any friends along the way.

I didn't mind hard training and like Biscuits I went away to win, but plenty of the Kangaroos saw him as unapproachable, unbending and some even thought he was unfair. We'd train twice a day and began every morning at about 7 am with a brisk walk through our tour-base neighbourhood of Leeds. It was never any different; from day one to the last day he was unrelenting.

Mind you, we had plenty of enjoyable times on that tour, too, as we did when we returned in 1982 and became tagged "The Invincibles". Some of the new players in the Australian team could not believe how tough Stanton was in 1982, nor would they believe it when we told them he had mellowed incredibly in four years.

Stanton's biggest problem was that he was abrupt with people. And he was worse when he'd had a few beers. He had coached Manly to a premiership in 1976 and '78; in '76 they beat Parramatta and in 1978 they won amid plenty of complaints from us, particularly over the refereeing of Greg Hartley. I don't think Stanton had much time for Parramatta, and after he had had a few beers, he left little doubt.

I had become a dual international in the 1978 series against the New Zealanders and it was obviously a very proud moment. After getting no further than Sydney Seconds in 1976 and '77, just as it had happened in Union all of a sudden I seemed to gain universal acceptance by the rep selectors. I played for Sydney Firsts, NSW, and then Australia in 1978.

We won my first Test 24–2 and went on to win the first three-Test series against New Zealand since 1967 by three Tests to nil. The side in my first Test match was: Graham Eadie, Terry Fahey, Mick Cronin, Steve Rogers, Kerry Boustead, Bob Fulton, Steve Morris, myself, Rod Reddy, Greg Pierce (c), Ian Thompson, George Peponis, and Graham Olling.

Bob Fulton took over the captaincy from Pierce for the second Test when Pierce was injured and retained it to lead the Kangaroos to England. Making their debuts with me in that first Test were Kerry Boustead, who was an amazing newcomer for Queensland in the interstate match, Steve Morris, a lightning-fast halfback from Wollongong who was an amazing bolter, coming from Country Seconds into the NSW side, and Manly prop Ian

(Magilla) Thomson, who had one or two great seasons with Manly as a ball player but never kicked on as many people thought he would. All of that side went on the Kangaroo tour except for Steve Morris and Terry Fahey, who had made himself unavailable before the side was picked.

In my books it was a magnificent Kangaroo side. The 1982 and 1986 squads may have gone through Britain and France undefeated, but I reckon the 1978 team would have beaten them both. Many people may find it surprising that I say that, particularly with all the hoo-ha about the next two sides being unbeaten, but club football was stronger in England in 1978. Sure, we lost both Tests in France, through diabolical refereeing and because, with the Ashes won, we relaxed. And admittedly, skills and fitness improved in Australian League in the 1980s, which gave the next two Kangaroo sides a bigger advantage over the Poms. But man for man, talent versus talent, the 1978 side was better.

As a guide, look at the *Rugby League Week* "Masters" side chosen in 1985. It was chosen by a panel of experts, including Stanton, as the best Australian side from 1970-85. In it were winger Kerry Boustead, a brilliant 19-year-old on that 1978 tour, centres Steve Rogers and Michael Cronin, the country's best centre pairing and right at their prime in '78, five-eighth Bob Fulton, the 1978 'Roos skipper who may have been near the end of his career but was still an incredibly competitive footballer with a wealth of experience, myself, and many claim I was a better attacking player in 1978 than in the '80s, and Max Krilich, our hooker, who went on to captain the '82 team.

As well as our "masters", there were Graham Eadie, a dynamic fullback who rates with Australia's very best and also at his prime on that tour, Craig Young, who played in all five '78 Tests and has probably never played better, Rod Reddy, who was certainly a better player in 1978 than 1982, Tom Raudonikis, one of the toughest competitors ever to wear the green and gold, and even a player like Larry Corowa, who didn't play a Test but in 1978 was probably the fastest and most elusive winger we had ever seen.

We won the first Test at Central Park, Wigan, by 15-9, but the Poms drew the series at Odsal Stadium, Bradford, when they beat us 18-14. The Poms played well in a really tough match, two tries were scored each, but as usual the Pommy referee, in this case Mick Naughton, gave the home side every chance. We won the series at Headingley, Leeds, when we flogged them 23-6. Compared to Tests

I practised my side-step a few times on the 1982 Kangaroo tour of England and France.

The 14th Kangaroos

these days it was a pretty spiteful series. I got head-butted by Jim Mills, there were a few brawls and Graham Olling was put out for weeks when he was kneed in the back. But in those days, that was the way Test football was played against the Poms. It was life and death.

It was the last season the Poms were anything close to being competitive against Australia, until in 1986 they showed some potential against the Kangaroos.

In 1978 Roger Millward was still skipper, and although he had been in Test football for a decade he was still a smart, hard-to-catch little bugger. Another player I had a lot of time for was John Joyner. Joyner was outstanding for England under-24s (even though we beat them 30–8) and was called in to the centres for the last two Tests. I thought he could have developed into something special; he toured Australia in 1979 and 1984, but never realised the potential I thought he had.

England's forwards were full of typically Pommie tough-men. Steve (Knocker) Norton was lock and they had blokes like Brian Lockwood, Phil Lowe, Len Casey, George Nicholls and big Jim Mills. Not too many of them were blessed with speed or fitness so they took us on in tight and tried to let the ball and their fists do the damage.

A lot of them toured Australia the next season when they were known as "Dad's Army". It was probably the worst British team I ever played against. They got stuck into the Aussie beer like their lives depended on it, apparently they slept in till 10 o'clock most mornings, and generally they were as undisciplined as any Pom team that toured here. The results in the Tests showed. We beat them 35–0, 24–16 and 28–2.

If they'd had Frank Stanton as coach, I wonder how many of them would have survived the tour. It is all right to socialise and we did plenty on the '78 tour, but when it came to training and playing every one of us was prepared to put in the work. Off the training paddock though, what a time!

I roomed with Steve (Hayseeds) Kneen. He went over with a knee injury from the grand finals against Manly, and played only six matches, but he probably saw more of Britain and Europe than anyone, except John Gibbs, that is. They went everywhere: West Germany, the Swiss Alps, and were forever going on day trips in England. Gibbs, the Manly halfback, should never have toured. Everyone knows that. He suffered a shocking hamstring injury in the semi-finals and was nothing but a passenger for the whole tour. None of the other guys minded. Gibbsy was a great bloke who fitted in well with everyone, but his going did show what a joke international medical tests had become over the years.

Even for Tests in Australia, it was only a case of coughing, being nudged in the ribs, lifting this leg, lifting this arm and you were passed fit. I've known a time when Tom Raudonikis, one of the toughest players I've known, could hardly walk. He'd put on an act as soon as he got within sight of the doctor, withstanding the obvious pain when he was examined, then declare he was right. And he would play five days later as if he was 100 per cent. On a three-month tour, however, things are a little different. Gibbsy was one of the worst examples of a player who shouldn't have gone, but eight years later a bloke called Steve Folkes also went away nowhere near fit, so times haven't changed.

There were plenty of characters in 1978. Rod Reddy never stopped playing practical jokes, the best (or worst) being when he shaved off Max Krilich's eyebrow one night. It all began in the foyer of the Dragonara Hotel, our base in Leeds, after the third Test which was played locally at Headingley. An English commentator was drinking with a big group of us in the main bar. He had a big handle-bar moustache and got so drunk he just about collapsed on the bar. Kerry Boustead wondered what he'd look like without a moustache and thought there was only one way to find out. So he got some scissors and snipped off one half of it!

A few nights later Rocket Reddy thought he'd try a similar trick with the Bomb Thrower (Krilich) and shave off an eyebrow while Krilich was asleep. Now Rocket was smarter than the average practical joker and thought he would nick a bit off his own eyebrow to suggest that someone had got them both. Well, the Thrower was furious and straight away suspected Rocket. And he vowed revenge.

On the way home after our ill-fated tour of France, we stopped over at Singapore. Rocket was flying straight on home to get married, so Krilich knew he had to get him back before Singapore. He talked Doc Monaghan (our medical officer) into giving him a sleeping tablet which he slipped into Rocket's beer, and you could see the tablet gradually taking effect, his eyes getting heavier before finally Rocket dozed off. The Thrower moved in, gently splashed some shaving cream over the eyebrow and was about to make his first stroke with the razor when Reddy opened one eye. Chance

Three Great Britain players attempt to stop me, but in a graphic illustration of what was wrong with English football at the time, not one of them had attempted to take me around the legs.

The 14th Kangaroos

lost! He had to wait four more years until the 1982 Kangaroos to get Reddy back, which he did.

Probably the two wildest characters were Tom Raudonikis and Queensland halfback Greg Oliphant. The pair roomed together and their room was permanently in a complete mess. There were half-eaten sandwiches and pies on the floor and under the bed, and clothes thrown everywhere. Once they threw a bed quilt out of the window and for two days it hung over two letters of the Dragonara sign at the front of an otherwise rather classy hotel. The pair used to have fights; one day it was stand-up stuff which nobody could stop. I really thought someone was going to get hurt, then next morning at breakfast, they were best buddies. Actually, it reflected how they treated their football. When NSW played Queensland, Raudonikis and Oliphant would give each other a terrible hammering, then that night they'd stagger out of a nightclub together, arm in arm, full of grog.

Quite a few of the players bought cars (more like jalopies) to get around in. Tommy picked up a little four-cylinder and took it everywhere, but I couldn't say he looked after it. One night we had gone to a pub on the outskirts of Leeds and as we walked out to go back "home" someone bet Tommy he couldn't put a keg through his own window. Tom picked one up and smashed it right through the windscreen of his car. Another time someone bet him he couldn't run over a tree on the side of the road. Tommy ploughed right over it. (Actually it was more like a thick bush.) Boys will be boys. It was all in together, which meant there was no room for wives on tour.

I found that out in 1978. My wife Chris and my sister Marilyn went over for a few weeks and stayed in Leeds, but not at the Dragonara. The only other wife to visit was Bob Fulton's Ann. I virtually had to sneak around like a Russian spy to get to see Chris. Wives were condemned; they were like a race from another planet, and were treated as if they had the plague. The thinking obviously was that the boys didn't want any outsiders knowing what they were up to and I got a hell of a razzing if ever I was caught in my own wife's company. In 1982 a few more of the wives went over, but certainly not mine.

We went to France at the end of the '78 tour, and it was a disaster. For starters, if we didn't speak the French language, generally they didn't want to know us. Secondly, their referees were the most one-sided in the world. They allowed the home teams to score tries over the dead-ball line, and they'd call us back for tries for "imaginary" forward passes. If the penalties were 5-1 the French team's way, we thought we were getting a pretty fair go.

The French played a fairly "unorthodox" brand of football. They were not violent in the sense that they elbowed and king hit. It's more that they played like girls; kicking, scratching and biting was more their cup of tea. Mind you, we weren't psyched up as well as we should have been for the final leg of the tour. We played six matches in France and lost three, including the two Tests, 13-10 at Carcassonne and 11-10 at Toulouse. It was the last time the French have ever beaten Australia.

It had always been the aim of Australian teams to get to Spain while visiting France, but the problems had always been the need for a visa to get across the border. And, naturally, to keep us out of mischief we were not supplied with visas before we left Australia.

In 1978 I told the guys I knew a place called Andorra which was an independent country where we could sneak across the border. I had a map of France and on it Andorra was only about 12 mm away from where we were staying. I'm sure the management knew we wouldn't get across, but they thought it would keep us out of trouble for a day so they let us use the bus driver and the bus for a day; quite a big group of the players took off. Being smart as usual, manager Peter Moore, the best Australian manager I've had, sent Doc Monaghan with us. We had to attend a function that night and the Doc was told to let us drive for a few hours and then tell Tony the driver to turn back.

So off we took, with a few cartons of warm cans to keep us occupied. After being gone for an hour or so we'd moved only about a three or four millimetres on the map. Little had we known the road went through a range of steep mountains and gorges and most of the way there was a drop of about 30 or 40 metres to a half-frozen river.

Anyway, when the two hours were up, Doc Monaghan told Tony he had to turn around and get us back for the function. To which the players stood on their feet, threw cans at the Doc and told him to sit down and behave. He didn't say another thing. After another hour we still weren't much closer to Andorra so we thought we had better turn around, but before we did I had a snap idea. In the river below us was ice, so why not we take the pillow slips off the cushions, climb down and fill them full of ice so we'd have some cold cans on the way home. Out we climbed and down we went. On the way we came across all sorts of things thrown over the edge of the road, among them was a baby's bath which came in handy as an ice bucket.

Needless to say it was an enjoyable trip home and then, as we reached the outskirts of Perpignan we came across a beautiful orchard, so we asked Tony to stop and we had a little picnic for about an hour. When we arrived back at the hotel we'd obviously missed the function. And we were in quite a state of merriment.

We lobbed into the foyer and ARL boss Kevin Humphreys was there, and didn't the fireworks start, particularly when we dumped our ice box and pillow cases in the middle of the floor and continued the party. Humphreys tore into Bozo (Fulton) who had been with us, and an almighty argument raged until Bozo was asked to go upstairs with Humphreys, Moore and Stanton. I thought Bozo needed some help defending himself so I followed shortly after to go into bat for him. It didn't go down too well and I was asked to leave. After it was all talked out, no official punishment was handed out.

The funniest thing was that Tom Raudonikis, who was usually the ringleader of such events, was one of the few players who had turned up to the function, and it seemed like he had made up for our absence with the amount of grog he'd put away and the entertainment he was putting on for our hosts.

It was a pity we ran into such horrendous refereeing on that tour, especially in France. The records show we lost six matches, three in England and three in France. Three of them were Tests. But in the games we conceded only 17 tries and in five of the six losses, we scored more tries than our opponents, which suggests what effect penalties, at convenient times in convenient positions, had on our results.

It was a fantastic performance really, even though we didn't make history like the next two Kangaroos. But Bozo's Roos were the best Australian team I played with.

The Invincibles

HISTORY UNFOLDED on the 1982 Kangaroo tour, but it went almost unnoticed by the players. The English public who flocked to the grounds to see an outstanding football team play, knowing it was going to be a one-sided contest against their locals, seemed to sense it long before we did.

Becoming the first Australian team in any sport to go through Britain undefeated was hardly discussed and certainly not consciously aimed at until we were a match away from doing it. We just tried to play as well as we could in every game. We never became overconfident although it was obvious the Poms had fallen so far behind us on the paddock. Then, the realisation seemed to set in before the third Test at Headingley. The press had been reminding us that no Kangaroo team had remained unbeaten. Our aim was simply to win the Test series 3-0. With one match remaining, it all added up to the same thing.

We'd won the first Test 40-4 at Boothferry Park, the Hull soccer club's ground. At Central Park, Wigan, we again won in a canter, 27-6, and that last Test at Headingley went our way 32-8. It was a game I watched from the stand because of a broken hand suffered in the second Test, which forced me to return a few days after the last Test for surgery in Sydney.

After going through unscathed in France this time, despite diabolical refereeing, the 1982 Kangaroos returned home as heroes, as The Invincibles. Like many things at the time, it didn't seem such a big thing, especially considering we were disappointed with the token opposition we had played. But, looking back, that effort seems more important.

The amazing thing on that tour was the English crowds. We picked up a cult following, people trailed us all around the north

The Invincibles

of the country like they would a rock band, just to see excellence. It was a magnificent side and the Poms allowed us to play open football. With our confidence up, we were able to do some incredible things. Even the London-based newspapers, who usually elected to ignore League for soccer and even Rugby Union, were carrying amazing tales of the Kangaroos. The whole of England sat up and took notice.

The backdrop of this chapter of history was again the Dragonara Hotel just near Leeds railway station, the coach was again Cranky Franky Stanton and nine players who had been there four years earlier had returned—Steve Rogers, Kerry Boustead, Rod Reddy, Chris Anderson, Ian Schubert, Craig Young, Les Boyd, myself and skipper Max Krilich.

Krilich deserved to go down as a history-making Australian captain. The Bomb Thrower was a great skipper who led by example and who had a terrific personality which made him popular and respected by everyone. He had a cool head and was as tough as they come. As a hooker I would have to rate him the best I played with. He never shirked his work, was fairly quick, had great anticipation from dummy-half, and he was strong.

It was ironic that two opponent hookers captained Australia almost straight after each other. Canterbury's George Peponis took over from Bob Fulton after the 1978 tour and after Peponis's retirement Krilich took the mantle, although Steve Rogers had the job for two Tests against France in 1981.

I've never thought that George Peponis should have captained Australia and will always regard his appointment as a political one to uplift the image of Rugby League. Peponis was a doctor and belonged to the proud Greek community. The Australian League, I reckon, thrust him forward as the respected citizen, the first doctor of medicine to captain Australia. While there it gathered a huge uplift of following from the Greeks, something that has continued to this day at Canterbury. Peponis was a good club footballer, a nice bloke and obviously a good skipper, but to me he was the Mike Brearley of Rugby League; never really good enough to play Test football but he went on to surpass that by being captain as well.

Krilich, however, measured up in every way, on and off the paddock. As in 1978, he, Rod Reddy and Ian Schubert were the ringleaders in all the off-field madness.

The Dragonara Hotel backs onto a canal and stands right beside a railway line. You walk from the hotel through a road tunnel under the railway and you are at the station and the edge of the business area of Leeds. The Dragonara stands on the main exit from the city to the M62 motorway which goes right across the north of England. Downstairs at the Dragonara is a casino, owned by Ladbrokes, who also own the hotel. The main lobby was on the third floor above two levels of carpark; there were a few lounges in the lobby where we could congregate, and to the left was a bar, to the right a restaurant.

Most of the "Drag's" floors were beautifully renovated, and very classy, except the eighth floor. That's where the Kangaroos lived for three months. The whole eighth floor was put aside for our 28 players, two to a room. If there had been any rooms left vacant, I doubt if the hotel management would have been game to house any guests there. Even our coach and managers stayed on a different floor, as did the Australian press contingent.

The lift doors on the eighth opened up to a small landing, and anyone who happened to get a glimpse of our floor when the lift doors opened would most likely have seen a game of indoor cricket, or darts, or a bout or two of rock-and-roll wrestling, or a few of our half-naked bodies roaming around. In 1982 there was an addition, a Packman video machine, and that electronic game became the centre of one of many tour incidents, one of which involved me as the villain. It was the one time, too, that I thought I was going to be sent home.

One afternoon Arthur Beetson, who had a supporters tour in England, dropped into the hotel and was playing the Packman with Sludge (Steve Rogers) and Les Boyd. To play the machine you had your back to the lifts, which opened directly behind. I thought it was the perfect setting for a bit of a practical joke.

That week we had picked up a few fireworks. They weren't the quiet, "pop" type, but super-dooper bungers. I decided to go downstairs, then come up a few minutes later and give Beetson, Boydy and Sludge a little surprise. The lift doors opened, but the three of them were concentrating so hard on their game they didn't seem to notice. With their backs to the lift, I pulled the bunger out of my pocket, lit the wick, rolled it just behind Beetson's feet and stood back in the lift to watch the action.

Big Artie jumped six feet in the air. He absolutely shit himself.

That, however, wasn't the end of the story. The smoke from the cracker set off the firm alarm. Mayhem broke loose. Everyone was

In enjoyed playing under Max Krilich, my 1982 Kangaroo skipper and the best hooker I played with.

The 1982 Kangaroos earned the tag, "The Invincibles" after going through its tour of Great Britain and France unbeaten. The new boys couldn't believe it when we told them that coach Frank Stanton (far left, middle row) had mellowed considerably in the four years since the 1978 tour.

evacuated from the hotel; from the rooms, the lobby, the bars, the restaurant and the casino downstairs. They couldn't use the lifts so there was a stampede in the fire exits. After I finished my laughing fit I looked out the window and realised what I had sparked. Six fire engines arrived and there they all were, standing on the street, Kevin Humphreys, pressmen, a few players and hundreds of residents. I thought if Humphreys found out what had happened I'd be on the next plane. Nobody dobbed me in.

Actually, I started a bit of a tradition with that prank. On the rest of that tour and in 1986 there must have been a dozen false alarms with the fire brigade, and mass evacuations. They became popular around midnight or 1 am. Everyone would be in their dressing gowns freezing on the streets when all was quiet on the eighth floor, most of the 28 Kangaroos tucked safely in their beds.

But there were times on the 1982 tour which weren't so enjoyable. One night when we were playing a game, someone decided to nick up to the eighth floor and thieve whatever he could from our rooms. Whoever it was got away with a bit of cash and plenty of souvenirs and left the locks on every room jammed.

Generally, the '82 tour was the same as '78—hard training, hard football and then a lot of fun and close mateship. And Stanton was much more relaxed, although still pretty tough. He seemed to be under less personal pressure. In '78 he had his wife with him. Maybe she put pressure on him. They were divorced a few years later.

Reddy was as usual the stand-up comic. And Eric Grothe played a mean guitar and could sing a bit. When we arrived we all chipped in to buy Eric a guitar so he could play on the bus. He didn't play once. The only time we heard him in concert was in the "brothel" of a room shared by Guru (Grothe) and Ian Schubert. Some mad things went on in that room, which became our most regular party venue. There were times when they'd be sipping champagne while standing on their heads. Another night we had a cigar party; everyone had to smoke a cigar. (Humphreys even joined in). The whole floor stank let alone Guru and Shoey's room. Other times you'd get out of the lift and hear the Grothe–Schubert duo in session. They even made a tape recording, but the "singing" was a bit suspect.

Others whiled away their time in the 24-hour casino down below. Peter Sterling, the keenest punter, spent half his time down there, and ARL officials Humphreys and Charlie Gibson regularly bet in big amounts. The most lasting memory of big Norths prop Don McKinnon on that tour was of him on the phone in the casino ringing home to Australia for more money. Others of us only dropped in occasionally; most of the blokes would reckon I respect money too much to have been throwing it away at the roulette table.

It was an eventful tour, historically, and also because one player left Australia as tour vice-captain but missed the Test side. It was Wally Lewis, who coincidentally roomed with Steve Mortimer. In the Tests against New Zealand in Australia, they were the half and five-eighth combination, but once the Tests began in England they lost their spots to my Parramatta team-mates Sterling and Brett Kenny.

Lewis and Mortimer were the terrible twins at first. Naturally they were angry at losing their spots and both claimed they didn't get a fair go. And they sulked about it for a while. Wally only had himself to blame. He was overweight, a lazy trainer and, compared to Brett Kenny (Bert), did not have the form on the board. When you go on a Kangaroo tour there are no mortgages on positions; Frank Stanton made that clear in 1978. Stanton paired Sterling and Kenny in the first '82 game, so they may have gotten the jump on Lewis and Mortimer, but the Sterling–Kenny duo was outstanding, so the lads got plenty of games together after that. Plus, Brett, Sterlo and myself were Eels team-mates and obviously blended well together.

I've always rated Kenny the better of two very good five-eighths. When it came down to two such evenly matched talents, attitude and form on the board obviously was going to be the difference. Bert won on both counts, despite Wally being vice-captain. By the time Wally stopped sulking and started to lift his game, it was too late.

I'm sick of people claiming I've got it in for Wally. I have never said he was not a great player, yet I have always claimed Brett Kenny was better. Wally has always been a lazy trainer and he feels because he's got such great skills and natural talent that he doesn't have to put in the hard work. If he did put in that extra work imagine what a magnificent player he would have been?

Steve (Turvey) Mortimer had an equally outstanding opponent for the halfback spot in Peter Sterling, who also had the form on the board. Turvey and Sterlo play different games and Sterlo's suited the English conditions better. I don't think Steve should have expected a walk-up start to the Test spot just because he played in the internationals at home that season.

Parramatta had a record six-player representation on that tour: Eric Grothe, Brett Kenny, Steve Ella, Peter Sterling, John Muggleton and myself (Mick Cronin was unavailable). It bettered the 1978 effort when I had Geoff Gerard, Ron Hilditch, Mick Cronin and Graham Olling as team-mates.

As it turned out, the 1982 side was an outstanding and perfectly balanced Test team. And when Wally Lewis finally made it into the side, as reserve in the last two Tests against the Poms, he played some superb football.

Mal Meninga and Kerry Boustead were the only Queenslanders in the first Test side. But any suggestion that Stanton favoured NSW players is as hysterical as the bullshit started by the Queenslanders over the dropping of four of them when Terry Fearnley was Australian coach in New Zealand in 1985. They have always wanted to cook up a conspiracy theory against NSW.

There was certainly no rift between New South Welshmen and Queenslanders on the 1982 tour. I roomed with Paul McCabe, and although he had the biggest inclination for sleeping I've come across, apart from another tour member, the big prop Dave Brown, McCabe was one of the nicest blokes I've met in football. Gene Miles became very close to Brett Kenny and Steve Ella, and Wally and Turvey were as thick as thieves. And Mal Meninga? You couldn't find a more easy-going person.

Big Mal blitzed the Poms. They hated tackling both him and Eric Grothe, who each scored some spectacular tries on that tour. If they kicked the ball to Eric it was suicide. Quite a few times in the club games he fielded the ball in his own half and pushed off tacklers like they were toys. Steve Rogers was the perfect link for Mal and Eric, while Greg Brentnall showed the best form of his career in England in 1982.

In the forwards there was size, flair and experience, even though there were only two players older than 30, Rod Morris and Max Krilich, Rod Reddy, whom many people thought was a shock selection, always seemed to reserve his best for Tests in England. Les Boyd, who ended up in the front-row, was outstanding and Craig (Albert) Young played some of his best fooball.

The Kangaroo's results in England were: 30–10 v Hull KR; 13–9 v Wigan; 29–2 v Barrow; 32–8 v St Helens; 31–4 v Leeds; 37–7 v Wales; 40–4, first Test; 44–4 v Leigh; 13–6 v Bradford Northern;

The Invincibles

41-2 v Cumbria; 22-5 v Fullham; 13-7 v Hull; 27-6, second Test; 19-6 v Widnes; 32-8, third Test. And tries were still only worth three points in those days.

We averaged crowds of 12,000, which was incredible. We scored 97 tries and conceded only seven in the 15 matches. I didn't go to France because of the broken thumb suffered in the second Test. I knew something was wrong when it happened, but I played out the match and was fortunate enough to win the man-of-the-match award. But X-rays showed up a fracture, so that was the end of my tour. Actually, the medicos nearly operated on my wrong thumb! I was in hospital and, just before I went under the anaesthetic, a male nurse came in and marked a cross on my right thumb. I told him, "You're not going to operate there." A bit startled, he asked why. "Because that's the wrong bloody hand you goose!"

I flew back on the same Qantas flight as Kevin Humphreys and Charlie Gibson. Humphreys was in first class, Gibson in business class and yours truly up the back in economy class. There is a moral there, somewhere.

We had to stop over in Singapore and I had so much luggage I had Buckley's chance of getting it through without paying excess. Humphreys fixed it up and put some of mine through first class with his. Then he fixed me up at a luxurious hotel where he organised a fantastic suite for me, while he and Charlie stayed in the penthouse.

Before leaving England, however, I took part in an incredible ritual that has become a tradition over the past three Kangaroo tours, including 1986. It took place behind the Dragonara Hotel. Like in 1978, many of the players pooled their money to buy old cars; Chicken George (Meninga) had a jalopy in 1982 which could only be classed as a bomb. It wasn't worth trying to re-sell the cars after the treatment they'd had, so they were either smashed up or just left there, but with Chicken George's a few of the blokes decided to do something different.

They wheeled it around the back of the hotel late one night to the banks of the canal, which was actually the Humber River running through Leeds, so it was pretty deep. A few of the guys picked up the car and hurled it into the canal in a "burial" service. We couldn't believe it but just as it started to sink, the headlights came on. None of us could understand why. Just then, some people walked around the corner and the headlights must have grabbed their attention. Everyone instinctively bolted.

Perpetual Motion

The people must have thought somebody was dumping a dead body in the car, because next thing the police arrived. When we woke up the next morning there were police divers searching the river and Bobbies going through the hotel questioning everyone. They never found the car which must have floated a fair way downstream. Mal admitted it was his car, but the police never found the culprits—who were out of the country a few days later.

Coach John Peard

THE FIRST NIGHT at training in 1980, John Peard gathered all the Parramatta players together for the initial big talk of the season. One of the first things he said was: "My name is John Peard. I know a lot of you call me "Scatty", but from now its John Peard or coach Peard."

I frowned. I hadn't called him anything but Scatty for four seasons. I just didn't think I could ever bring myself to call him "coach Peard". It went against everything I had become accustomed to. And that was the biggest problem for John Peard when he went from team-mate to coach in one hit. I think he would admit now it was the worst thing he ever did in his career, particularly as it was at the same club where he had played. The people he had played with were not going to treat him seriously enough, or with the necessary authority, particularly when there were so many long-term "legends" like Arthur Beetson and Bob O'Reilly.

None of this had anything to do with any lack of ability John Peard had as a coach. When I played with Peardy I always thought he would be a great coach, and to be honest, I was asked my opinion of him becoming coach long before he was appointed. I suggested to secretary Denis Fitzgerald that the club should go for Peardy, but I didn't see the warning lights at that stage.

Peard had every attribute to be a young Jack Gibson. He had played under Gibbo's coaching in two premiership-winning sides at Eastern Suburbs. He was a great tactical player, a great kicker, was perfect in defence, a good communicator, very popular as a clubman and a very keen trainer. He had the right attitude for Rugby League, but he was a man out of his time. He was meant to be a coach, but not at Parramatta in 1980.

I certainly don't blame the coach that the only time Parramatta didn't make the semi-finals in the dozen years from 1974 was in

1980. Nor was that year a failure. We were right up there within two points of the competition lead until the last three premiership rounds. And we had won the Tooth Cup, Parramatta's first "official" title in first grade. (We'd won the Wills Cup pre-season competition in 1975.) Our being in the Tooth Cup final obviously was part of the reason for our dreadful finish to the premiership, but that's only my impression as a spectator, because I missed the cup final and the end of the competition because of a knee injury.

Just the same, I thought it was a bad move giving Peard the reins from Terry Fearnley so soon. Some people claimed that giving him the reserve-grade job first might have been a better solution, but that still wouldn't have avoided the same problem; Peardy would have been coaching his team-mates because he played a fair bit of reserve grade in his last season while he was battling a chronic groin injury.

Many critics, from within the club and from outside, reckoned senior players like Beetson, O'Reilly, Geoff Gerard and myself were running the side, but that's not true. It was obvious Arthur had a pretty big influence on what Peard did, and sure it never seemed as if the coach had the ultimate authority, but Beetson was a legend and the most experienced player in the club. And he had coached first grade himself, when he was player-coach of Easts in 1977–78.

Right through the season it seemed that only Arthur Beetson or Bob O'Reilly would be in the side at any one time. Peardy persisted in dropping O'Reilly to make way for Beetson, who spent plenty of time out injured, even though I thought the Bear was playing better football. It was as if Peard thought he was obliged to pick Arthur because they were such close mates and because he was a legend. It must have been hard to drop a legend, but that was what Arthur Beetson was.

Arthur Beetson didn't come to Parramatta in 1979 until he was well into his thirties, but he still had "it", that charisma and ball-playing ability few others have had. He wasn't fit in 1980 and I think he was finally given the ultimatum to get himself into shape or else.

In 1979 he was reasonably fit and really started to make a difference to Parramatta until he broke his jaw, ironically against his old club Easts. There was nothing vicious in the tackle by Gary Metcalfe, but Arthur trooped off Cumberland Oval with his jaw badly dropped. And that was it for him that season.

Coach John Peard took the job before his time. His eyes stay on the action while conditioner John Healey tends Geoff Gerard.

Perpetual Motion

By the next season his wonky knee had started to give him more trouble then ever before, and he had trouble getting on the paddock each week. But when he did, he was still good. Beetson was a good talker, he had a great ability to read the play, and he could see things unfolding when others couldn't. I enjoyed playing with him.

Bob O'Reilly played a similar style. He was a great off-loader, although he didn't quite have Beetson's ability to slip the ball from an impossible position no matter what stage of a tackle he was in. Generally the Bear had a better season than Arthur, but in that year I remember two great games Beetson played. One was the Tooth Cup final against Balmain.

Parramatta was pretty much understrength. I'd been out for weeks with a knee injury and the weekend before, Michael Cronin had been sent off in a spiteful match against Wests. We couldn't believe it; the fairest player in the game being sent off? It showed how spiteful the game had become and how much unfair attention he had received. Eventually Crow retaliated and he and Ted Goodwin were both sent off after a flare-up.

O'Reilly was also out, and we'd brought in Michael Collins, for his first game in the top side, to fill in as a goalkicker while Cronin was out. Collins scored all our points from four goals and we won 8-5. Beetson had a blinder, he took it up to the Balmain forwards all night and slipped some magic balls.

Only a few weeks before, Beetson, who was then in reserve grade after coming back from injury, was a shock selection to captain Queensland in the first ever State of Origin match, played at Lang Park. I missed the match with the knee injury, but I remember watching it on television and I had never seen Beetson come out so fired up. His eyes were lit up, and he was so pumped up it was as if he was on angry pills. And he played angrily too. He chased Mick Cronin all over the paddock, he hunted him, and got him with a couple of good ones too. I couldn't believe it was happening. Queensland won and Beetson was the hero. Only a few weeks later he finished his Sydney career in the reserve-grade grand final, which Parramatta lost to Canterbury 18-16 after extra time.

For the first-graders, however, the season had finished three weeks earlier, in one of the most disgraceful efforts by a Parramatta team in my years there. The competition ladder that season was incredible. With three rounds to go the table read like this: Wests 26, Parramatta 24, Easts 24, St George 24, Manly 24,

The Bear, Bob O'Reilly, and I after I had broken his record of 216 first-grade games with Parramatta. Bear and I both had bars named after us at Parramatta Stadium, though I reckon O'Reilly, as Parramatta's first junior to play for Australia, deserved to have his name on the grandstand.

Steve Edge coming over the top as I stretch out against St George. Later we were team-mates at Parramatta and he was my skipper when we won the premiership in 1981, '82 and '83.

Coach John Peard

Canterbury 24. That meant five teams were two points off the competition lead, yet one of them would miss the semi-finals. It was to be Parramatta.

We lost our last three matches. The Sunday before the Tooths Cup final we were thrashed by Wests 34-9; the big night-match was obviously in the back, or maybe the front, of our players minds. The Sunday after, backing up from the glory of winning the Tooth Cup, we were beaten by Canterbury 15-14. Which meant that in our last match, against Saints, the winner would go into the semi-finals and the loser was gone for 1980.

I had made myself available for the Tooth Cup final after being out for a month, but the doctor ruled me unfit. If we had beaten St George, I would have been fit to play in the semi-finals, but we went down to the Saints, 20-11, at Cumberland Oval. Parramatta played with no authority. Saints gave us no respect. It was terrible; we surrendered with hardly a whimper. After being up in the leading bunch all year and only a few weeks earlier looking at winning the cup and fighting out the minor premiership, we missed the cut off.

The year will go down as a bit of a disaster for Parramatta, even though we won the cup. But it was an even bigger disaster for me because of injury. I vowed then that I would win a premiership and a Wednesday night cup before I finished.

I also lost the Parramatta captaincy that year. Critics were claiming it had been affecting my form and that I was stood down, but the decision was mine. If I had been asked to give it away or been told it was affecting my form, I wouldn't have given it up. It would have made me even more determined to keep it.

I had taken over the captaincy from Ray Higgs at the start of 1978, under Terry Fearnley. I enjoyed the captaincy, but only a few weeks into the season I was under fire from the media, who claimed I should have given it up because they thought I was losing my cool. I was a very aggressive person and I didn't control myself at first, and I was accused of making a few bad decisions, particularly when I elected not to take goalkicks on a couple of occasions, but those critics didn't know what was happening on the field. If we got a penalty I would ask the goalkicker, normally Mick Cronin, what he thought. Could he kick it? Would the ball go dead if he didn't? Or was it better to keep the pressure on the opposition by attacking their line? There were other situations when the opposition deliberately conceded a penalty so they could slow the game down and regroup in defence. They were prepared to give us two points instead of six (or five as it still was in those days when a try was still worth three points). I had to make many quick decisions and obviously sometimes I would be proved wrong.

At the start of 1979 I was under the most pressure. We'd won only one of our first four games and the critics were again calling for my blood as captain. They claimed those of us who had gone on the 1978 Kangaroo tour were stale, and the captaincy was an unwanted burden. Eventually we got our act together and we made the semi-finals. During those two years, 1978 and '79, when my captaincy was continually under fire, I became a Test player, toured with the Kangaroos and won the Rothmans Medal as well as other player awards, so I will not agree that it affected my form. The greatest pity was that I ended both seasons in the stands, after being sent off.

I retained the captaincy when Peard took over as coach in 1980, but I was serving suspension at the start of the year so Ron Hilditch filled in. Then I went away for several weeks with the Australian team to New Zealand and missed more club games. When I returned I had a broken thumb as well, so I told Peardy that it was better for the team to keep Hilditch as captain. He'd had the captaincy more than I had anyway, and had done a good job, so it was better for the stability of the team for him to keep it. As it turned out, only a few weeks later I did my knee ligaments and didn't play again that year.

Denis Fitzgerald had become club secretary by then, and it was a move which got plenty of support from the players. Fitzy was always a bit of leader when it came to players' rights during his playing days, and when he took over from Bob Jones, a good bloke who, however, was never seen as a driving force in the club's progression, the general attitude of the players was "you beauty". That was the start of 1979. Fitzy had only given the game away at the end of 1977 at 27; he'd been playing firsts since 1971 and virtually was sick of playing, although he had also had to put up with coeliac disease for a few years. It had made him run down for some time and when it was diagnosed it meant there were things he couldn't eat or drink, including beer, of which he had a fondness like most players at Parramatta. So Fitzy became a white wine man.

During the two seasons we played together, Fitzy and I had become quite close. When I first came to the club he was more or

Coach John Peard

less the one who made me feel welcome and he took me under his wing a bit. Often after a game the players had to pair off at the Leagues club to sign autographs and mix with the supporters. Fitzy and I, and our wives Sandra and Chris, would stick together. We had some great nights, me having a few beers and Fitzy hopping into the wine—he could put a few bottles away.

Unfortunately, in the latter part of my career, when I was captain and Fitzy was secretary, things were not always that happy between us, but Fitzy made an instant impact on the club when he started as secretary and is largely responsible for the modern success of the Eels. One of the big things he did in that first year was to attract Jack Gibson to the club. It was during the semifinals in 1980, before we'd come to grips with missing the finals, that he was announced as Peard's successor.

The news certainly received a mixed reaction within the club. Gibson had an incredible reputation as a motivator, as a winner, and as a very tough man. I'd met him only a few times in the previous few years and I found him a very quiet man, but he had an aura about him and an air of fear, particularly for players.

I'd heard a lot about him and my first reaction was one of curiosity. There was a question in my mind about what it would be like to play under this unique coach, who was already seen as one of the greats. Then I thought what a challenge it would be, and I became very keen to play under him. He was known as a hard taskmaster who ran things his way or else. Obviously it scared some others off.

A heap of Parramatta players cleared out before Gibson got to Parramatta. Geoff (Jethro) Gerard went to Manly. He felt he had been at the club too long and needed a change, but Jethro was a bit lazy on the training paddock and I think Gibbo scared him a bit. I thought Jack Gibson could have made a great player out of Geoff Gerard had Jethro stayed at Parramatta. Graham Murray (Little Artie) and Micheal Pattison went to South Sydney, Graham Olling went bush, John Chapman and John Mann took off for Brisbane, and Glenn West went back to Penrith. Then, after Gibbo started, Lew Platz and Mark Levy were cut a week before the 1981 competition began, and both ended up at Penrith. So it was the end of one era and the start of another for the Eels.

The pre-Gibson era had some good players and different personalities. When I joined Parramatta, John Quayle, later to become general manager of the NSW Rugby League, was the lock, in many ways my predecessor when you look at long-term permanancy, although he spent a lot of time in reserve grade in 1976 while I was biding my time in the second-row. Cannon Quayle was a pretty quiet bloke who was very popular. He was working as assistant manager of Eastern Suburbs Leagues Club although playing for Parramatta. Before I arrived, he had come home from the 1975 World Cup with a crook shoulder which never really recovered. It was my practice in that first season, as it has been since, to watch the reserve grade and in particular to see how the lock was going, to see what pressure was being put on me. What I remember most about Quayle was that when he and halfback Terry Reynolds played in reserve grade they were the best pair I had ever seen when it came to the old set move of switching the ball back into the lock from the scrum. They scored a string of tries using the ploy.

During 1978 and '79, before Peter Sterling became a regular in firsts, we had Graham Murray as one of the most unlikely looking halfbacks in the game. But he was a wizard when it came to reading the play and setting up his supports. He was always a little lazy, and I have vivid memories of him turning up to training in his panel van, dressed as if he'd slept in his clothes, or simply in his swimmers. He'd grab anything he could find in the back of the van to train in.

There were plenty of characters, but some of them wouldn't have survived under Jack Gibson. A lot left at the end of 1980, but there were plenty of promising young players coming through, and one of the main things Gibson was renowned for was discovering young talent. He didn't miss at Parramatta.

Jack Gibson and Success

JACK GIBSON was not the best coach I played under. But Jack Gibson and Ron Massey were the best coaching combination I played under. Gibson is called the "master coach", but that is only half the truth. He would never have been as great without his right-hand man Massey. Both were brilliant minds who complemented each other perfectly, and together they provided the edge Parramatta needed not just to win our first premiership, but to put three together from 1981-1983.

I was fortunate to play under some great coaches at Parramatta—Terry Fearnley, John Monie, and even John Peard would have proved a great if given the job at the right time. The difference between the rest and Jack Gibson was Ronald Massey. If Terry Fearnley had had a right-hand man, or an extra gun on his belt, he too would have gone down in history with a record similar to Gibson's. That is what Massey was to Gibbo, the gun on his belt, and in many ways his eyes and brains.

Jack Gibson was a very smart man, and a very smart coach. He was the front man of the operation. He spoke his own language; sometimes he talked in riddles, other times he could not be more to the point. But much of the analysing, the strategy, and the detailed homework was done by big "Mass", who will go down in the League record books as a mystery man, an unsung hero.

Gibson has an unmatched record in the modern era. He had brought Eastern Suburbs from the wooden spoon to be semi-finalists in 1967 and went on to win five premierships. He had had the ammunition each time and probably landed at Parramatta at the perfect time. There was a deal of uncertainty at Parramatta when the man who was a legend in his own time was announced as the new coach in September. It was still only October when he got us together for the first time. Nobody knew what to expect.

Perpetual Motion

There was curiosity mixed with fear in some players' minds; they knew that from now on there would be no room for half-hearted effort. We all expected to have our bums trained off by a dictator, but we were wrong.

I'd met Jack Gibson a couple of times earlier. The first time was at a Caltex–Sun sports star night in 1974. Arthur Beetson won the award that night. Gibbo knew who I was, even though I was still playing Union, and naturally I knew who he was. In a group, we struck up a conversation and to be honest I thought then he was a bit strange. He was talking in his riddles. But in his three years as Parramatta coach, I found him to be very shy, yet a very caring and generous person.

As a coach he did a lot of things others didn't or wouldn't, but the great secret of his success was that he and Massey were more thorough than the rest. Their basic formula was simple: they put the onus on the players. If we wanted to succeed, it was the players' contribution that would lead to it. He preached self-discipline, self-pride and the golden rule was that there were no short cuts.

A normal week under Jack Gibson was packed solid.

Tuesday: We were expected to have treated our own injuries suffered in the previous weekend's match. We arrived at training about 5 pm and played cricket until we started training at 5.30. First was the team talk, each team going over the previous Sunday's match. Gibson and Massey went through the main points of the match, assessing each player's performance, listing his mistakes and his good points, and giving him a rating out of 10 points.

If you were to be dropped you would be notified privately and given the reasons why. Gibbo never dropped a player on one bad game, giving him the benefit of the doubt. Two bad games in a row, though, and that could be different. He had a pretty blunt way of letting you know what he was about to tell you. He had his particular sayings like, "Do you know the reserve-grade coach" or "Do you know that boy Jimmy Bloggs in reserve grade, well go and get him."

We then came together as a club and announced all the awards from Sunday's match: the game balls for each grade and any other awards. And birthdays for the week were announced and then the teams would be read out. Massey always stood behind Gibbo, and it was almost as if he was a ventriloquist. He knew everything Gibbo had to say and any time Jack stumbled on his words or paused, Massey would pick him up.

Jack Gibson and Success

Next, we hit the paddock, did our warm-ups and then got into our skills training, drills with the ball and tackling bags.

Thursday: We all were expected to have done some sort of fitness training by ourselves on Wednesday. When Thursday came it was straight into the warm-ups and then into the ball work and our plans for the coming match. Gibbo trained us with the ball until Massey came out to tell us the time. We usually went for about two hours, but if Massey was yapping away and forgot to come out and tell Gibbo the time, Jack had us out there for two-and-a-half, maybe three hours. Before we left we each got our match plan or "tip sheet". Massey would have watched our opposition's previous couple of matches on video and listed some of their regular plays, their tap moves which they might have scored off, their dangerous players, who to watch from dummy-half, and who their kickers were. We often discussed the points, or we were just handed the sheet and expected to read it.

Saturday: We trained at 8 am; just a light session with warm-ups and a run down of our plays for the match and our general moves. After that was the club barbecue, and by then everyone was prepared for the next day's game. Gibson's motto always was that the preparation was done during the week, not on match day. His coaching virtually stopped on Saturday morning. There was no use hitting us with last-minute instructions or big psyche sessions minutes before kick-off. If we weren't prepared mentally and physically during the week, we weren't going to be on the Sunday.

The team barbecue was always a source of fascination for me. If Gibbo and Massey stayed to eat, we had to have half as many sausages and steaks again as usual. They could eat, especially Massey. He'd keep stuffing it down his throat like it was a bottomless pit.

We didn't see much of Gibbo before the game on Sunday; he came in for a brief welcome early, we got dressed and went for our warm-ups, and he just reinforced things with us before we ran out.

Gibson was fortunate he had so many young and talented players ripe for the picking when he came to the club, players like Brett Kenny, Peter Sterling, Eric Grothe, Paul Taylor, Steve Ella and John Muggleton. Gibbo was perfect at making young players realise their full potential. Wherever Gibson has been, there's been a heap of talent, and what he's done has been to aim them up, send them in the right direction and give them some help along the way. He put the onus on them. It was as if they were all rough diamonds

Perpetual Motion

which just needed polishing; some of them might have cracked along the way but they all were still polished up with a nice sheen.

And he wasn't averse to trying things other coaches wouldn't. Over the past two decades, Jack Gibson has been as responsible as anyone for changes in the game. One gamble he took in 1981 proved a real winner. He took Paul Taylor, a halfback in under-23s, into the first-grade pack even though Squizzy was only 67 kg (10½ stone). Taylor wore the number 10 jersey, but he played lock, with me going into the second-row. To be honest, I had a superstition about wearing another number on my back and I was the Test lock at the time and didn't want to give the rep selectors any ideas. Taylor was an amazing success. Pound for pound, kilo for kilo, he was the best footballer I played with. He was an inspiration. On his day he was just all enthusiasm and used to bring down the big forwards by wrapping himself around their ankles. In the mud at Cumberland Oval on May 31 that year, he set a club tackling record of 52, which still hasn't been beaten. Squizzy later went on to be the regular fullback at Parramatta and added a bit more finesse to his game, but back in 1981 it was Gibbo who recognised his heart and not his size.

Gibbo had a couple of players in his first year at Parramatta who weren't so young. Plenty of the critics panned him for expecting to get mileage out of two old "crocks" Kevin (Stumpy) Stevens and Bob O'Reilly and plenty of them claimed if there was room for one of them, there definitely wasn't room for both. Gibbo loved putting egg on faces and that's what he did when Stumpy and the Bear played vital roles in our grand-final victory over Newtown.

At first I wondered what Jack saw in Stumpy Stevens. He'd been around for a while and was virtually playing on one leg when Gibbo brought him from Easts. I soon found out what he saw in the nuggety back-rower. Stumpy was a winner. He trained his butt off, he had a huge heart, an abundance of enthusiasm, an insatiable will to win and a great tolerance to continual inconvenience. That attitude rubbed off on everyone, particularly the younger blokes.

Stumpy used to limp around all week because of his knee and often couldn't do a full training session until Saturday or Thursday. But the knee rarely stopped him, and once he got on the paddock, he gave nothing less than 100 per cent effort. The way he hit in defence was unbelievable. He had ball skills and what he

Jack Gibson and Success

lacked in mobility because of his crook knee he made up for with sheer determination. I have a lot of admiration for that old "crock" called Kevin Stevens.

The rebirth of Bob O'Reilly was also another Gibson-Massey coup. And few people realise the Bear had to overcome a shocking ankle injury along the way. He had the worst ankle I've ever seen on a footballer. His head wasn't much better. At times he could hardly walk, let alone play football, on his ankle, but Gibbo had instilled that desire in him that had never been there before. He always had the Bear on the scales and off the grog to curb a weight problem that had always been with him. They rode him all season, but the effort was worth it.

Jack Gibson was good for every one of us. He changed my attitude in one way. I was hot-headed and aggressive, but Jack taught me to channel that aggression into more beneficial outlets. If someone belted me on the field I would usually retaliate, and go looking for them. I had a tendency to argue with referees and at times got frustrated and lost my cool. Gibbo took me aside and told me it was the same with him: "they" didn't like us. I suppose by "they" he meant the opposition, the crowds, and the referees, who were trying to encourage me to do silly things. If I struck for the ball in the play-the-ball, 10 times out of 10 the refs penalised me because I was Ray Price. Players chased me and belted me and if I retaliated I would be the one to get punished by the referee. "They" were going to do me no favours, Jack said, so I had to control my aggression and frustration. I had to put extra effort into the next tackle, Gibbo told me, and say "that was for Joe Blow". I had to put in that extra effort to show they couldn't get to me. It was good advice and I think after a while I got it right.

I was captain in 1978-79 and the first part of 1980. Steve Edge, a hooker from St George who joined Parramatta in 1980, was made captain ahead of Ron Hilditch and me in 1981. Jack didn't ask me if I was disappointed in not being captain, but he more or less talked around the subject. He explained he needed several "captains", and assigned players to marshal specific areas on the field and at training. We had four "teams" within the club, each with a captain, and there were different contests between the teams, which included players in all grades, taking in such things as our time trials, sprints, and punctuality. There was a presentation for the best team at the end of the season.

Gibbo also explained that for the first time in his career he had

Perpetual Motion

13 players capable of winning the man-of-the-match award each week. He'd already won two premierships with Easts and they were regarded as the greatest club side of the '70s, so it was quite a statement.

Jack saw the leadership qualities in Steve Edge as being probably more beneficial than his qualities as a player. I remember a lot about the St George players in the late '70s, but I remember little of Edgey. He was a plodder, a player who did his work and went unnoticed, an efficient dummy-half, and he came up with plenty of tackles. As a skipper he had a settling influence, rarely becoming flustered. And he got plenty of assistance from Mick Cronin in the backline and with experienced forwards like O'Reilly, Stevens, Hilditch and myself around him. Edge will go down as captaining four first-grade premiership sides, St George in 1977 and Parramatta in 1981, '82 and '83. It was a feat to be proud of.

We made the pre-season final in 1981, losing to Easts 12-3. (It ended up being the last pre-season final because when Canberra and Illawarra were added to the premiership the next season, there was no time for an organised pre-season competition.) We beat Newtown 33-9 in the first premiership match and I, for one, certainly didn't expect to be playing them in the grand final in September.

Steve (Zip) Ella made his return in that first match which was a miracle. Zip had been out 18 months after having a complete reconstruction of his knee, and it was generally thought his career was over. He always hung around on his crutches and turned up at every match. We all were willing him to come back but no one was sure if he would. When he scored five tries in the first three matches of the season, he left no doubt that he could pick up all the pieces.

A player who had taken just as long to come back to form got busted again early in 1981. Peter (Wally) Wynn suffered a serious knee injury which put him out for the season. Further injury troubles played on him for a few more seasons and it probably wasn't until 1985 when he played for Australia, that Wynnie regained his confidence.

His problems began at Cumberland Oval in 1979 when Cronulla's Kurt Sorensen belted Wynn behind play, and escaped being sent off for it. Wynnie suffered bruising of the brain and was out for 14 weeks, yet it took years before he was anything like the same player again. (He had played for NSW in 1979, his first

There were some great days during Parramatta's winning seasons under Jack Gibson.

season at Parramatta.) He seemed to pull out of matches for little things, and would never take the paddock unless he was sure he was 100 per cent fit. In Rugby League it doesn't matter how physically fit you are, if you're not fit mentally you're gone.

Wynn showed a lot of persistence over the years with the head injury and two serious knee operations, but inconsistency was his main problem, even in 1985 when he wore the green and gold. He had a great match for NSW Country to make the NSW side and then had a blinder in the first State of Origin to make the Australian side. Then he played pretty well in the first Test, but he didn't do a lot more that season. If Peter Wynn stopped cutting in on plays and running across field, and instead ran straight and hard, he would have been one of the best players NSW ever produced.

Back in '81, after a bit of a slump in the first round, we won eight games straight and knew it would be our premiership, even though the critics were still at us. We drew the last premiership game 18–all against Manly in what ended up being the last match played at Cumberland Oval. That dropped us to third spot behind Easts and Newtown. We knocked off Newtown 10–8 in the semifinal and only had to beat Easts to make the grand final. The Roosters had beaten us three times during the year but we were mentally stronger, and came out in front 20–8.

Everyone expected Easts to climb back and still win the premiership, but Newtown shocked them in the final and the Jets, whom we had beaten so convincingly in the first match of the year, stood between us and history on grand-final day.

It was more a case of Tommy Raudonikis standing in our way, because he was the heart and soul of Newtown that season. He was the driving force behind the Jets, not coach Warren Ryan. I've always thought Ryan was a bit jealous of Tommy's incredible stature and the way the younger players looked up to him, and it's interesting that towards the end of that season he kept taking Tom off in matches and replacing him with Ken Wilson.

There were no holds barred with Tommy, an old mate from the Australian team. In that grand final I belted him and he bit me back. He bored it up us and when we seemed to be getting the upper hand, Tommy scored a try through sheer determination close to the line. The Jets got their tails up and I think they thought they had it won. Luckily we fought back and two tries by Brett Kenny sealed the game.

Jack Gibson, a genius coach at the spiritual home of Rugby League, the Sydney Cricket Ground.

Perpetual Motion

I'd come off with a crook ankle and the Bear, ugly ankle and all, was sitting with me on the bench when the hooter sounded. The Bear grabbed me and started hugging me and then he put aside all the pain of his ankle and ran onto the field to greet the other players. My first reaction was to look towards the Hill, to all those Parramatta fans who had waited so long. We had all been trying since we'd begun our careers at Parramatta, but many of those fans had been waiting a lifetime for their team to become the champions. And they went crazy.

As I had driven to the SCG (the rest of the players went in the club bus), I was the first player back at the Leagues club that night. I thought I would sneak in but it was impossible. Chris and I were mobbed. Once inside, there was standing room only and you couldn't hear above the noise. Eventually the players, officials and our partners were able to get away from the mob to celebrate by ourselves.

It was a long night and being hidden away inside the club it wasn't until the next day that we realised the crowd had burnt down Cumberland Oval. It didn't alarm us because we were all expecting work to begin any month on the proposed Parramatta Stadium. Little did we know what that night of drunken behaviour by some of our fans would cause: a weekly hike to Belmore and training sessions at Granville Park.

Granville Park was a joke when we started there in 1982. Once a month I would trip in a hole and twist my ankle. There was talk about having it resurfaced but it never happened. We used to get quite a crowd at training and it became impossible to have our team meetings in the little open stand, so Jack Gibson bought a bus. At first vandals kept breaking in and wrecking it, smashing all the windows and ripping the seats. Our sponsors, Hardies, fitted it out with Hardieplank and they put bars on the windows and it became our home away from home for four years. At first I used to sit up the back of the bus and muck around a bit, but when I became captain under John Monie I had to progress to the front and be the one to tell the lairs up the back where I'd once sat to be quiet.

Gibbo, who was a pretty wealthy man, bought that bus himself. It was one of his many acts of generosity. He was a generous, lovable person, and a lot of people didn't see that side of him. One player had trouble getting to training because he couldn't afford a car, so Gibbo bought him one and let him pay the money back at

Jack Gibson and Success

his own rate, without interest. Whenever a player's wife had a baby, flowers were sent to the hospital from Gibbo and Massey. If there seemed to be an off-field problem worrying a player, they would try to help out. They wanted all players to be employed. If you were not, the word would get to Gibbo and he'd ask around and try to line something up for you.

We won two premierships from Granville Park and Belmore Oval. I regard 1982, when we beat Manly for the first of two times, as my first "real" grand final. I didn't complete the match in 1981 and being there at the finish was what it was all about. The 1982 win was more important to me even though 1981 was the club's first.

In 1982 and 1983 Manly knocked us off in the major semi-final, but were no match for us when it counted. I honestly thought both times they were overconfident and had played their grand final two weeks too early.

In '82 they flogged us 20-0 in the semi, but as I walked from the SCG I knew they could not possibly have played any better while we had a heap of improvement in us. We beat Easts 33-0 in the final to earn a rematch with Manly in the grand final. In the decider, when Neil Hunt dropped a bomb over our line for Phil Blake to score, Manly thought it was only a formality again for them. We came back to win 16-3, even though referee John Gocher hammered us with penalties.

The next year Manly were minor premiers and we had to beat Canterbury to play them in the major semi-final. It was one of the most exciting, open games I've ever played; we beat Canterbury 30-22. The game will be remembered for Eric Grothe's amazing try, when he beat seven defenders in a 40-metre run that started on the right touchline and ended up beside the posts—it was one of the best I've ever seen.

Manly again went into the grand final first, after beating us 19-10. We had to play Canterbury again, beat them 19-4, before we got another crack at Manly. It's easy to say now, but I always knew we had Manly's measure, even though they beat us in the semis both years. They had no chance in the '83 grand final. We scored two tries to lead 12-0 after 13 minutes, and led 18-0 early in the second half. We won 18-6.

The hatred between Manly and Parramatta had subsided a fair bit by 1982. And I didn't think the Eagles were a very tough side mentally. When their confidence was up they looked like world beaters, but when the going got tough players sometimes seemed to be looking to their team-mates beside them for inspiration. That's the trouble when you buy so many superstars. One bloke thinks of the other, "You're getting paid $50,000, why don't you get us out of trouble?" It's still the same now. It's usually Des Hasler or Paul Vautin who are left to take the initiative when things aren't going well.

Those early 1980s were fantastic for Parramatta—three premierships in a row. We were the first club to achieve the hat-trick since St George's record of 11 straight.

Jack Gibson went down in history as the triple-crown coach, and Steve Edge as the three-times winning skipper. Ron Massey's name might be missing from the record books, but all of us at Parramatta recognised his contribution. I've never met anyone like the man. He had that individual touch and all the answers. He was like Gibbo's private secretary, his personal diary. And he knew a footballer as soon as he set eyes on him. Along with that, he had an incredible sense of humour and a great turn of phrase. Probably the funniest prank ever played at Parramatta was from his planning.

In 1981, Bob O'Reilly was due to play his 200th first grade match. Massey thought he'd organise a special presentation at training, which ended up being a set-up. He arranged for Michael Cronin, who got on incredibly well with the Bear and was always mixed up in some mischief with him, to make the presentation after training on the Saturday. The Crow made a lovely, moving speech and the Bear, at first staggered to see his mate so serious, was close to tears. Then he gave the Bear a watch in a beautiful case. Everyone cheered and the Bear responded with what, for the Bear, was a touching speech.

Over the barbecue, the Bear was on cloud nine. He said to Massey how great it had been that all the fellas thought so much of him, and he wondered how much the watch had cost, how much we had spent on him.

Well! Massey grabbed the watch, called the Bear an ungrateful bastard and yelled about how these blokes had dug into their own pockets to give him something and he was worried how much it cost. His final salvo was, "Stuff you Bear" and with that he dropped the watch on the ground and smashed it to pieces, stomping on it three times.

The Bear went white. He blurted out, "But, but, but," as he

picked it up in a hundred pieces. The whole place turned to a stunned silence. I don't think anyone but the Crow and Massey knew that it was a cheap Casio watch which had only cost about $10. The Crow couldn't control his laughter, but when the prank was finally explained, the Bear wasn't impressed. Later we presented the Bear with a dinky-di watch.

From Big Jack to Little John

JACK GIBSON had never stayed at one club for more than three years. He felt that he would have given that club all he could in that time and it would be time for someone else to take over. He told Steve Edge, Michael Cronin and me before the 1983 grand final that he was likely to leave Parramatta. But a certain Parramatta official made up his mind for him.

Gibbo didn't have much time for this one official and he and Massey, like a few others, found it hard to work with him. The crunch came on the 1983 grand-final night, back at the Leagues club.

The players always attended an official function upstairs after we had done our bit with all the supporters. Gibbo had asked a couple of friends to join us at the function, which he was quite entitled to do as coach, but this official wouldn't let them in and there was a bit of a scene outside the door. I think that was the last straw for Jack, even though he had enjoyed his three years at Parramatta more than any other period in his coaching career.

Jack had told Edge, Cronin and me that if he left Parramatta he would never coach a team against us while we were playing. And he made that public at a function at Oatlands Golf Club a few weeks after the grand final. That night was a memorable one for all the players because it was an unofficial farewell for Gibbo and Massey. They presented every player with a plaque which listed the squad, and each player's "title" under the banner of "In Appreciation—Jack Gibson—coach—1981-82-83 championship squad".

My line read: "Ray Price, team captain, charitable works, media liaison, demonstration officer." The "charitable works" was because I was known for counting my money and always trying to help the players make some of their own; "media liaison" was because most of the media were scared to approach me and probably didn't like me; "demonstration officer" had me a bit puzzled, but probably had something to do with me always arguing on behalf of the players with club officials, and "demonstrating" their cause.

It was a really clever bit of literature from Gibbo and Massey. Massey came under the classification of "catering co-ordinator on all forms of gluttony". Peter Sterling had the words "turf investments" (he was a mad punter), "house securities" (his house was always getting broken into), and "need to have a hat shortly group" (in reference to his thinning hair). Michael Cronin received the honourable mention of "diving on the ball instructor" (he was rarely known to dive on a loose ball) and "sniff dog attendant" (he had a terrible habit of always sniffing).

The four team captains, Steve Edge, Peter Sterling, Michael Cronin and I, also received framed photographs of a group of players holding up the Winfield Cup after the 1983 grand final. It was another little thing which made Gibson and Massey different to the others. After coaching a side to three premierships it would normally have been the coach who received something from the players. Gibbo and Mass wanted it the other way around.

Jack sat out the next season, but was back into coaching at Cronulla in 1985. If he meant he wouldn't coach against Edgey, Crow and I while we were playing as a group, he stuck to his promise, because Steve Edge retired at the end of 1984. He had suffered a shocking eye injury in the 1983 grand final against Manly, and it looked like his career had ended there and then, but he showed plenty of courage and tolerance to stick it out and although the vision in his eye was never right again, he got a clearance to come back towards the end of the first round in 1984.

But if Gibbo meant he would not coach against any of us while we were at Parramatta, he didn't quite stick to his word. Not that any of us minded. He was a wasted talent sitting at home on a Sunday, or watching football without any involvement. As it was he came back to coaching only after some prompting from his long-time mate Terry Fearnley. My first League coach was at Cronulla in 1983 and '84 and felt it was time to give away full-time coaching. He desperately wanted Gibbo to take over the reins because he knew how much potential was in the club, although they had plenty of financial dramas at the time. I think the challenge appealed to Jack all along, to coach his "local" team. (He had lived near Cronulla for years.) Just as it was when he joined

Parramatta, he knew there was a heap of young talent to develop; it took a bit longer than he was used to, but in 1987 the Sharks started to really blossom under Gibbo.

Wherever Gibson coached, he insisted on selecting his own staff, his minor-grade coaches, conditioner, medicos, the lot. In 1981 he discovered a bloke called John Monie who had a very impressive record with Woy Woy on the Central Coast. Jack had never met Monie, but had done his homework on him and decided he was the man he wanted as understudy, as reserve-grade coach. Gibbo wasn't wrong with his judgement very often and certainly wasn't in this case.

When Gibbo leaves a club he likes to have some say on who his successor should be, and naturally his opinion is widely respected. He had earmarked Monie and had groomed him from the start in 1981. Actually Gibbo made a comment right at the start of that first season which highlighted what he thought. He apparently told the committee about Monie, "This bloke should probably be coaching first grade, not me. He's won more pennants than I ever have."

Monie had a couple of seasons as a nuggety little five-eighth with Cronulla in 1967–68 (with Canterbury coach Warren Ryan as a team-mate) before going back to the bush. As coach and captain-coach with Woy Woy, he had won four premierships in six years. It took him the same number of seasons to get his first title for Parramatta—and to finally get out of big Jack's shadow.

In presence, Gibbo and John Monie were poles apart. Jack was a giant with an aura of fear and respect. John was a little bloke who certainly had respect, but was younger and in some ways was one of the boys when he was reserve-grade coach. It was obvious to me who was going to get Jack's job long before Jack's leaving was even made official. He made John Monie more involved in our preparation during the final series in 1983, using it as a bit of a settling-in period.

John Monie was his own man. He naturally continued a lot of Gibbo's ideas, thinking obviously that when you're on a good thing, why not stick to it. And Monie didn't want to walk in and make his changes just for the sake of leaving his own stamp on the club. But he was a different man and a different coach.

It was a pity we missed out on our fourth successive premiership in 1984. Even though we went so close, only a Michael Cronin goalkick away from going into extra time, Monie was the coach who had to carry the stigma of being the one who'd failed after Gibbo had taken us to three straight titles. If Jack Gibson had stayed one more season, maybe we would have won in 1984, but I say that with no disrespect to John Monie. Monie was in his first year of Sydney first-grade coaching and couldn't have been expected to give us the edge Gibbo might have done.

It must be remembered that Canterbury, who beat us 6-4, were the strongest side Parramatta had played in a grand final at that stage. Manly might have had more superstars in their line-up in the two previous years, but as a team they weren't a patch on Canterbury. We went into the 1984 grand final after losing prop Geoff Bugden the previous week with injury. Then Steve Ella went off hurt in the opening minutes. It was one try each but we lost by a goal, so there were no shortcomings in our coach.

Monie didn't shake off Gibson's shadow until we finally won another premiership in 1986. Gibson, with his great reputation, had come to Parramatta and in his only three seasons guided us to the club's only first-grade premierships. In the eyes of many of our supporters, and the media, Monie was like the batsman who came in after a Bradman double century, and could not hope to match up to the great man before him. John Monie and the players never thought of it that way, but it was a stigma Monie had to live with. In the end that was as big a driving force for me as anything else; to bring him out of Gibson's shadow once and for all. He deserved it. He stands up there with the very best of the modern era.

When we beat Canterbury to take the 1986 grand final in my last match, the first thing I did was look for Michael Cronin, then other players bandied round us and lifted us onto their shoulders to take us towards the presentation dais. John was standing quietly, letting us soak up all the attention. I walked over to him and said something like, "You can stand on your own now." And he could.

In my last season Monie and I had become fairly close as a coach-captain combination. He respected my opinion and often called me into discussions on team selections. We ended up with a very close and strong working relationship, and strangely, it evolved from a talk we had in 1985, when I had wanted to punch him in the nose.

It was only a few weeks before the semi-finals. At training on the Tuesday night John called me into the bus for a private discussion as had often happened. His first question was, "How

I've always wondered how the opposition lock or halfback saw me!

All dressed up with no place to go, except to the ground. The headgear wasn't there to conceal my receding hairline, but to protect a nasty gash on my forehead.

important is the captaincy to you?" It took me back, and straight away I was on the defensive.

"It's very important to me," I replied. "It is one of the goals I have set myself. Something I have always wanted to do is to captain Parramatta to a first-grade premiership. Why?"

The coach told me he thought Peter Sterling should be captain and that I should give it up to concentrate on my game. Sterling, as a play-making halfback, called most of the plays and I led by example and made the decisions when needed. It was a system that seemed to work well but we had become an inconsistent side in the second half of the season and were looking at going into the semi-finals from fourth spot.

The first thought that went through my mind was how the two "old blokes", Cronin and I, had given it everything when six of our top players were in England for the first two months of the season. We had built up such a fantastic spirit then. Since the topliners had arrived back from overseas (Sterling was one of them), we had lost our consistency, and it seemed I was to blame.

I felt like a knife had been thrust in my back. I didn't know what to say or do. I told John Monie that if he wanted to give Sterlo the captaincy I would give him my total support, but I wanted him to know that I was dirty that he had done this to me.

Monie must have changed his mind because I stayed as captain for the rest of the season, although I thought that when 1986 began, Sterling would be captain for sure. Nothing more was said and John Monie and I seemed to be even closer and able to understand each other better than before. He knew how much I treasured the captaincy and I knew I had to do that little bit more to keep his faith.

As it turned out, 1986 became the greatest season in Parramatta's history. John Monie mightn't have brought home three premierships in a row, but he was the only coach in the history of the game to win a National Panasonic Cup, the Giltinan Shield, the minor premiership, and the club championship in the one season.

On top of that achievement, John Monie was a very sincere person. Like Gibson, he never appeared emotional, and rarely raised his voice. He always seemed under control. Most times he outwardly appeared quietly confident about himself, but other times you could tell he was a bit unsure. He had his little favourites, his idiosyncracies, but unlike Gibson, he didn't have a right-hand

John Monie with me on our glorious grand-final day in 1986. No wonder we were all smiles. I was so glad he had finally shed Jack Gibson's shadow.

man and would rather sort his problems out himself or, I'm proud to say, he would ask and respect advice from his captain and senior players. He never thought it showed up any insecurities if he asked others; it only showed he was human and was sincere in trying to get the best results for the club.

In an interview when the Eels weren't going that well in 1987, John Monie called himself a "coach of consistency". He said he wasn't into trick plays or magical cures, and that it was up to him and his players to perform consistently under pressure. That, he thought, was the sign of a good team.

Those words really summed up his attitude and how he regarded himself as one of the team rather than a level above his players. That was always how I saw him, although he knew that he was the boss and it was his head that was on the chopping block when things went wrong. Like Gibson, he wanted to be in control of his own destiny so he relied on his own instincts and his intimate knowledge of his players.

Monie also picked his own staff. Bert Bass, who coached the under-23s when Gibson was there, had the under-23s up to 1987, when Bob O'Reilly took over. And Peter Louis, a mate of many years from Woy Woy, took the reserves. Monie and Louis had played together when they were in their late teens. Both went to play in Sydney, John at Cronulla and Peter at Canterbury, and ended up eventually back at Woy Woy together, John as first-grade coach and Peter as both reserve-grade and under-18s coach over the years. When John went to Parramatta in 1981, Peter took over the top side at Woy Woy, and when Gibbo left in 1984, Louis and Monie joined forces again. Obviously there was a lot of trust between them because they had been through so much together, and like Monie before him, Peter Louis was regarded as a very good reserve-grade coach who should end up in first grade one day.

Coaching reserves is probably the worst job in the world. There is always a last-minute change in the first-grade line-up, which means the reserve-grade coach loses a player with little notice. There is inevitably a player or two who has been dropped from first grade and feels he shouldn't have been, and the reserve-grade coach has to cope with that too. At Parramatta we had so many representative players, someone was always being called up from the seconds to cover for them when they were away. However, one thing at Parramatta was that the seconds coach always had plenty of outstanding young talent to work with.

From Big Jack to Little John

Neither Monie nor Louis won reserve-grade premierships. Parramatta's last one was in 1979. Both of them got to the grand final after being minor premiers, Monie in 1981 and Louis in 1986. John Monie made the progression to the big league without any worries, though, and now has a much deserved premiership medal in his trophy cabinet.

I was fortunate to play with the very best coaches of the modern era—Fearnley, Stanton, Gibson, Beetson and Monie. On performance only Bob Fulton, who has never won a premiership, and Warren Ryan would rank with them. But I don't think I would have enjoyed playing under Ryan.

None of them had a season as successful as Monie's in 1986. For a little man, he can certainly stand tall.

War Games

I WATCHED the first State of Origin match at Brisbane's Lang Park in 1980 on the television set at home. It was like watching a war movie. And English referee Billy Thompson didn't do much to defuse the war. It was like an England–Australia match of years gone by, except the players were all Aussies.

I had played in the first "legitimate" interstate match that season and scored two tries in NSW's 35–3 win. Then I tore my knee ligaments and missed the second clash, which we won 17–7. They were typical scores since I had first played for NSW in 1978; Queensland had never beaten us in that time and since 1975 we had won 14 out of 15, the other being drawn.

When I saw Arthur Beetson, my Parramatta team-mate, lead Queensland out on that night of July 8, 1980, and then tear into the NSW side as if it was World War III, I could tell Australian Rugby League was in for its biggest change.

Beetson charged round the place, incited an all-in brawl, and harassed Michael Cronin, another Parramatta mate and the fairest player in the game, like there was no tomorrow. And his Queensland team-mates followed like men inspired.

The Maroons, boosted by Sydney-based players Kerry Boustead, Alan Smith, Greg Oliphant, Rod Reddy, Beetson, John Lang and Rod Morris, won 20–10. It was two tries apiece, but a big young centre called Mal Meninga kicked seven goals for Queensland. His centre partner, who looked more like a prop who had drunk too many schooners, carved us up out wide and won the man-of-the-match. His name was Chris Close.

I would have liked to have played in that first "origin" match, even if only to give the Crow a hand. But you could tell, even from watching on TV, these games were going to be different to anything else Rugby League could offer.

War Games

Within three years State of Origin matches between NSW and Queensland had become the toughest and highest level matches in the world. I regarded them as the best, Test matches next, then grand finals, Sydney club matches and finally Sydney versus Country in order of quality.

In State of Origin matches the 26 best players in the world fight it out for 80 minutes as if their lives depended on it. Test matches have become 13 of the world's best versus five world-class players plus a few who weren't quite up to the top standard, yet the chance to wear the green and gold of Australia still holds number-one pride and place. For the ultimate football experience on the paddock, however, it is Queensland versus NSW at Lang Park.

Beetson's boys stored up all their hate and all the frustration of being continually on the losing side for that first night in 1980. From the next year Beetson became coach, but the games didn't become any easier.

In that first year it was decided to have a fully "origin" match only if the usual series had been decided after the first two games. With most of Queensland's best players in Sydney, it was only a formality that NSW would lead 2-0.

It was the same format in 1981 and with the same result. NSW beat Queensland locals 10-2 and 22-9, then the Maroons called in their reinforcements from Sydney for the third match and it was war all over again. That was my first taste of State of Origin football and it's a night I'd rather forget.

We led 15-0 after 28 minutes, with all the points scored by Parramatta players. Eric Grothe had scored two tries and Micheal Cronin had scored a try and three goals. The game was won, or that's what a few of the NSW players had thought at least. We had some inexperienced players and their greenness certainly showed. Our prop, Steve Bowden, who fancied himself as a tough guy and used to shadow-spar in front of a mirror, decided to go after Queensland's Rod Morris at every opportunity. Second-rower Peter Tunks had a shocker and hooker Barry Jensen kept dropping the ball. Poor old Terry Lamb was called into the team on the morning of the match for Micheal Pattison, who had to withdraw because of sickness. Wally Lewis, in his first game as captain, played all over him. You can't underestimate Queensland's determination, but to let them come back to beat us 28-15 was one of the most pathetic collapses I have ever been involved in. Some of our blokes had their minds on other things and I ended up letting my frustrations go by head-butting Chris Phelan in one of the most stupid things I've done on a football field.

When the three-match interstate series became a fully State of Origin one the next season, the Queenslanders had already posted wins in both previous "origin" games. Their dominance continued in my remaining three seasons of representative football and in the eight matches I played, we won only two. Naturally, I didn't like to lose that often.

I have certain theories about why Queensland dominated in those first few years. Firstly, their preparation was usually better. They came together prior to the weekend before the game, which was played on Tuesday nights, and all their players, Brisbane- or Sydney-based, were rested from the previous weekend's club rounds. We had to play on the Sunday, bash the you-know-what out of each other, and then back up two days later for an even harder match.

Also, Queensland settled on a side very early and kept it together for quite a few seasons. That was the advantage NSW had in the late '70s; what was virtually the Test side would come together and we'd have a very good understanding. But after State of Origin football started, the NSW selectors seemed to want to chop and change, and with only a couple of days together before the interstate matches, we seemed to be playing into Queensland's hands.

Queensland had players like Wally Lewis, Mal Meninga, Chris Close, Kerry Boustead, Paul Vautin, Greg Conescu, Mark Murray, Wally Fullerton-Smith and Colin Scott, all of them internationals, together almost from the start.

I didn't have a big respect for too many Queenslanders as individuals, but as a unit they combined into a great side. They had more desire and when they put on that maroon jumper, they seemed to become men possessed. I'd sure like to know what they were fed before those games. There were blokes like prop Dave Brown, whom I had never fancied much as a player. Brownie would be in reserve grade in Sydney, then he would be called into the Queensland team and improve 150 per cent. The other guys around him seemed to lift him, plus he was able to get away with a lot more than he could in the Sydney competition, which suited him. Dave Brown went on to play for Australia on those few good performances he put in for Queensland.

Another thing against us was that we always played two matches

War Games

at Lang Park and one in Sydney. I was always dirty on that. The only reason for it was because the League could get its hands on more money through the television rights to be had by beaming it live from Lang Park back to Sydney, rather than what could be got for telecasting it from the SCG to Brisbane's smaller audience. It was typical. Money ruled the League's thinking. It showed a disrespect for the people who turned out at the SCG to support their team and a disrespect for the NSW players. We always got a percentage of the gate receipts but we never saw any of the millions they got from television over the years.

Lang Park could be a harrowing experience for younger players, and we fielded plenty in those first few seasons. But, I absolutely loved playing up there. A big crowd always lifted me, even if it was right behind the other team. I never found the Lang Park crowd spiteful; it was a good mob of people who booed you and hated you when you wore a blue jersey, but who also got right behind you when you were playing for Australia. I played some of my best games at Lang Park and I won quite a few man-of-the-match awards up there.

When we got to the ground in the NSW bus, they'd just stare at us and yell out "C'mon Queensland" or something worse. If we stood out the front of the stand or sat down while the curtain-raiser was on, often some of the people would come up and ask for our autographs or to have a chat. Other times they'd just stare at us as if we were something strange. But there was rarely any abuse, and they'd never yell out "I hope they kill you" or "I hope you break your jaw", which happened from time to time at Sydney club games.

Once we got halfway down the tunnel to run on the field, the boos would break out. We could hear it come from the stand on the other side of the field first, and by the time we were out under the floodlights, the whole ground was booing. They wanted our blood, but as far as I was concerned they had to come and get it. It was them versus us and it just spurred me on.

The one advantage the Queensland team had was they really felt at home there and Wally Lewis seemed to know every blade of grass on Lang Park. His kicking game there was unparalleled in Rugby League and according to the Lang Park crowd he just couldn't do anything wrong.

They called Wally the "Emperor of Lang Park" and he won so many man-of-the-match awards I honestly thought it must have

Wally Lewis gives the gesture to the SCG crowd. They have given him heaps over the years, but the "Wally sucks" chants were a bit unnecessary.

been written into his contract. I think Wally was embarrassed at times to pick up the awards, but it was just because of the almighty pedestal he had been put on by Ron McAuliffe and the media.

I remember vividly the match in an absolute quagmire at the SCG in 1984, when Queensland beat us 14-2. Greg Dowling was by far the best player on the field and scored a freakish try when he scooped up the ball in the wet on the half-volley after it had rebounded off the crossbar from a Wally Lewis kick, then dived over for a try to clinch the match. Who got the man-of-the-match award? You guessed it, Wally Lewis.

It wasn't just the Brisbane press who thought he was greater than God. Most times when he won his regular man-of-the-match award the Sydney press guys far outnumbered the Brisbane contingent. It got to the stage where, if there were five passes leading up to a try and Wally had thrown the first pass from dummy-half, the media, particularly one TV commentator, would most likely say it was the magic pass from Lewis that set up the try.

You can't blame Wally, he was just playing the game, but the pedestal he had been put on certainly created problems for him over the years, and made him very sensitive.

Wally has mentioned in his memoirs that he thinks I have a God-given right to criticise people. It's possibly because when I'm asked to comment on something or someone, I don't beat around the bush. I know I'm not very diplomatic, but I am paid to pass comment in *Rugby League Week* and I give them as I see them. I speak what I think is the truth and if the truth hurts, that's someone else's bad luck, not mine. It's a big boy's game, and if you can't swim you shouldn't go in the deep end.

Wally is in the deep end now as Australian captain and it's about time he started fluttering those arms. League is a high-profile sport and if you can't accept criticism, it's time to get out. He hasn't learned to accept that, probably because of that pedestal I've been talking about. He either thinks he's above criticism, or he's just not used to it. Either way he doesn't handle it too well. If there's one thing you have to be able to do in League it is to give and take. Strangely, Wally has said it's never been his go to "bag" anyone publicly. I was surprised, then, when he dropped the bucket on a heap of people to the author of his recent biography.

Wally Lewis, despite all the controversy, has been a great player. When it comes to State of Origin football, he has been sensational. The more NSW has tried to spot him, the more he's starred. He stands deep and so wide he's like a centre, not a five-eighth. I've played against him and it is sometimes impossible for the lock or the five-eighth to get to him, particularly with Mark Murray inside throwing the long passes as well. But Wally is not holier than thou as he has been painted and as plenty of people have tried to make him out to be.

It's a pity most of my State of Origin memories aren't good ones. The only wins I had were 20–16 at Lang Park in 1982, and 10–6 at the Sydney Cricket Ground in 1983. And there was plenty of controversy in those first few seasons of "origin" football, just as there is now.

There was the infamous pass by Phil Sigsworth to Moree winger Phillip Duke in the deciding game at the SCG in 1982. Like everyone else, I couldn't believe it when Siggy threw the ball behind his line, Duke spilled it, and Lewis came through and scored. It cost us the game 10–5. I remember being behind the tryline while Mal Meninga was lining up the conversion, and Max Krilich and I were telling our players not to worry, what was done was done. We just had to concentrate on getting back into the game. We couldn't blame Sigsworth and Duke. They didn't mean to blow it.

There was that tackle by Les Boyd on Darryl Brohman at Lang Park in 1983. Brohman busted his jaw and lost whatever chance he had of playing for Australia, and Boyd was put out of the game for a year by judiciary boss Jim Comans. I was moving in to tackle the player who was to receive the ball off Brohman. At first the tackle didn't look too bad and I thought that when Alan Thompson landed on top of Brohman as he hit the deck, more damage might have been done. But when I saw the replay that night it was ugly alright. It was frightening.

There was also the match when Steve Ella was chosen as five-eighth, but the day of the game coach Ted Glossop switched him with Alan Thompson and made him reserve. I was mad about that. I have always wondered if it was Glossop's idea or whether he was being influenced by the selectors, or someone else. Ted wasn't a very radical or authoritative sort of bloke and it surprised me that he would do such a thing. You can't choose a player for NSW and then turf him before the match. Glossop called Ella aside during the day and told him he was putting Thompson in; I think he simply told him he thought Steve would have a much bigger impact as a reserve than Thommo would. As it turned out, Lewis and big Mal Meninga ran roughshod again, and Thommo, a great organiser and team player, just wasn't dynamic enough to worry Queensland. When Zip Ella finally came on in the second half he scored a try, but we were already gone and eventually lost 24–12.

My last two games for NSW were in 1984 and nothing had changed. We lost 29–12 and 14–2, and Wally Lewis picked up both man-of-the-match awards. Barry Gomersall refereed my last, in the mud at the SCG, and when you talk about Queensland's success in State of Origin, Gomersall should get a mention. He certainly was more lenient than Sydney referees, particularly when it came to a bit of biff, and he suited the Queenslanders more than us.

I have to take my hat off to Queensland, however, for its determination and obviously fantastic team spirit. When the state got the use of its Sydney-based players for those one-off matches in 1980 and '81, they were able to call on the improved skill, fitness and dedication those players had learned in Sydney. The local boys then lifted their game around them. One of my regrets was that I had finished, a bit prematurely thanks to the selectors, before NSW had lifted the level of its preparation and determination to be right back there, above them, again.

Farewell Australia

Most people would have thought it was an ironic sight—Wally Lewis chairing me off the Sydney Cricket Ground after my last Test in 1984. We'd had a few digs at each other in the newspapers and it ended up being a pitched battle between Wally and I for the Australian captaincy for that season's series against Great Britain, but Wally and I got on quite well in each other's company and as players we had a big respect for each other.

I had said at the start of 1984 that whoever won the first State of Origin match should supply the Test captain. I made no secret of the fact I dearly wanted to captain my country, but I was quite happy to abide by the umpire's decision. As it was, Queensland won the first interstate match and Wally got the job, which he held right through to the 1986 Kangaroo tour, becoming only the second Queenslander to receive that honour.

Wally didn't have to make peace with me or ask for my support in that 1984 Test series. I was vice-captain and was naturally going to give him all the support I could. We were playing for our country, and I found Wally Lewis a darn good captain to play under.

It's funny how it worked out that year. Queensland got the captain and NSW got the coach in Frank Stanton. Queensland should have had the coach too. Arthur Beetson was hard done by in being stripped of the job after having it for the two Tests against New Zealand the previous year. It was as if Artie had been blamed for the loss to the Kiwis at Lang Park, Australia's first loss in 17 Tests. Arthur should have been given another year, particularly as Stanton had resigned from the job the previous season and was only coming back for one year. (It looked as though Stanton was asked to return.) Terry Fearnley took over in 1985.

It wasn't Arthur Beetson's fault we lost to the Kiwis in that '83

Farewell Australia

Lang Park Test. For starters, the New Zealanders were able to bash the hell out of us with little action from English referee Robin Whitfield. Judiciary chief Jim Comans had had a big cleanup of foul play in Australia, and a lot of our players were naturally shell-shocked when the Kiwis turned it on. Kurt Sorensen, in particular, tore right into us.

I know it will sound biased, me being from NSW, but we had too many Queenslanders in the side. Brad Tessmann, in his Test debut, had his jersey knocked off, which naturally put him off his game a bit. He had to run out in the number 17 jersey. A couple of others were struck by a virus, but naturally didn't want to miss out on playing for their country and declared themselves fit. And there were others who were supermen in State of Origin games, where they gave life and limb, but just weren't able to put that effort in again when it came to Test football. They weren't tried and true, and if you look at the side and how many of them failed to kick on in Test football (Scott, Tessmann, Fullerton-Smith, Brown), it speaks for itself. The team was: Colin Scott, Kerry Boustead, Mal Meninga, Gene Miles, Eric Grothe, Wally Lewis, Steve Mortimer, Ray Price, Wally Fullerton-Smith, Paul Vautin, Dave Brown, Max Krilich (c), Brad Tessmann. Reserves: Dave Brown, Steve Ella.

New Zealand had developed a very good side under Graham Lowe. Where we had widened the gap in standard between us and the Poms, New Zealand had narrowed the gap between themselves and Australia. They had improved their skills and experience through having most of their team playing club football in Sydney or England. They really took it to us in that game and I thought a few of the Australians turned it up a bit.

The Kiwis' 19-12 win was Max Krilich's last Test and it was a big disappointment to all the Australians that he had to go out that way. But for New Zealand it was the greatest boost of confidence they had ever had. They finally proved to themselves that they could beat the mighty Aussies, and I have seen that confidence in them every time they have taken on Australia since. They should have beaten us 3-0 in the 1985 series and would have done except for some bad luck and two miracle escapes when John Ribot scored last minute tries for Australia in the first two Tests. The Kiwis thrashed Australia 19-0 in the third.

New Zealand has become a much tougher opponent than our traditional rivals, the Poms, but the side the Brits sent out here in

Perpetual Motion

1984 was a great improvement on its previous few teams. The Poms seemed a much more dedicated side and they had a fair bit of pace in the backs and muscle up front. Still, we beat them 3-0 in the series.

The Great Britain side to take us on in the first Test at the SCG was: Mick Burke, Des Drummond, Garry Schofield, Keith Mumby, Ellery Hanley, John Joyner, Neil Holding, Mick Adams, Andy Goodway, Chris Burton, Lee Crooks, Brian Noble (c), Keith Rayne.

Unfortunately that Test will mostly be remembered for the blatant elbow, one of the most savage I have seen, by Pom reserve David Hobbs on Greg Conescu. It was one of the lowest acts I have seen on a football field and I think even his Pommy team-mates were dirty on Hobbs for his disgraceful act.

I suppose that Test will also be remembered as the only one played by Ross Conlon, who came into the Australian team amid a heap of controversy at the expense of Eric Grothe. I felt sorry for Ross because it wasn't his fault he was in the side, even if it was only to kick goals. Mal Meninga was hurt so Ross, who was really a centre and not a winger, was slotted in to kick goals. The selectors couldn't put him in ahead of Brett Kenny and Gene Miles, so Eric was given the flick. I wouldn't say Ross Conlon didn't deserve to play for Australia, because goalkicking is a big part of the game and he was the best in League at that stage. I must admit, however, I didn't think we had to have a brilliant goalkicker because Wally Lewis was a kicker of some note and I thought he could have handled the job without any worries. But the selectors obviously expected it was going to be a very close Test and they didn't want to take the chance.

I thought Ross Conlon was an under-rated player in those days, when he was at Canterbury, although he seems to have been much more highly rated since he's become an important member of the Balmain side at centre. He is aggressive, deceptively quick, and strong. As a goalkicker I rate him, together with Mick Cronin, as the best I have seen. To be perfectly honest, he was a good club footballer whose goalkicking skills opened up further doors for him.

That first Test team to play for Australia was: Garry Jack, Ross Conlon, Gene Miles, Brett Kenny, Kerry Boustead, Wally Lewis (c), Mark Murray, Ray Price, Wayne Pearce, Bryan Niebling, Greg Dowling, Greg Conescu, Dave Brown. We won 25-8.

Farewell Australia

Eric Grothe was brought back for the final two Tests, but hasn't played a Test match since. Guru could have been the greatest winger Australia had ever seen, but he was his own worst enemy and has never had an attitude to match his ability. In the past few years the selectors have obviously thought twice about choosing him because of his injury problems, and it all came to a head in 1986 when he was ruled out of the Kangaroo tour at the last minute because the League doctor, Bill Monaghan, thought his knee was too suspect for him to tour. I don't know who was right or wrong there because I've heard so many different stories, but obviously Monaghan was reluctant to send anyone away who wasn't fully fit, remembering John Gibbs and Steve Kneen in 1978. He had already ruled Wayne Pearce out of the 1986 tour a few weeks earlier. My only question was why Steve Folkes had been allowed to go when his groin was obviously not right.

Grothe always seems to have been worried by injury. A knock on the knee or a hard tackle is all it took to put him out of action. Peter Sterling, playing for NSW Country, brought him down in the game against Sydney at Newcastle in 1986 and Eric limped off with a crook knee which put him out for weeks. Eric has never trained as hard as he should have and he has never seemed mentally 100 per cent. He just never fully dedicated himself towards being the best. But what talent!

He was so strong and fast with a close-to-the-ground running style which allowed him to crouch in tackles and bump off his opponents. And he has pulled off some of the best cover tackles the game has ever seen. He was the perfect, natural footballer. The pity is that the public have never seen the real Eric Grothe, and I doubt that they ever will.

As a person he would do anything for you and was a real easy going spirit. He told me once in about 1979 or '80 that he was thinking about giving up football to concentrate on his music. He was a good guitarist and could sing a bit. I said, "You're mad Eric. How are you going to make the same sort of money or future out of music? Unless you are the very best in the music business, not many doors are going to open for you. Look at yourself and your future." Luckily he reverted to jam sessions in his garage.

The Poms hated playing against him and 1984 wasn't any different, although he didn't seem to get a lot of the ball. The English side was a lot fitter than usual on that tour and although we won quite handsomely, when you look at the scoreboard that

I swapped jerseys with Wayne Pearce after my last Test in 1984. It was my farewell gesture to Junior Pearce, who had always been heir apparent to my Australian lock position. However, I have always believed he was better suited to the second-row.

Wally Lewis and I doing some warm-up exercises at Australian team training. I never minded Wally's company and enjoyed playing under his captaincy. I simply objected to the superhuman pedestal he had been placed on.

Wally chairing me off with Wayne Pearce's assistance, after my last Test at the SCG. Ironic?

first Test was pretty tough and we looked forward to an even tougher second Test in Brisbane. Australia won that one 18–6, but I watched it on the old colour TV because I was forced out with a calf-muscle injury and replaced by Paul Vautin. Unfortunately Fatty Vautin broke his cheekbone in that Test and I slotted straight back for the third at the SCG. It was to be my swan song.

Wally Lewis and Frank Stanton let me lead the side out that day. It was a nice gesture. I had scored a try in my first ever Test (for Australia in Rugby Union in 1974) and was determined to score a try in my last Test match as well. Unfortunately I tried too hard and ended up running around like a headless chook. We won a rather tame Test 20–7 to take the series 3–0, and I ended up winning a radio station's defensive award, which was nothing but a sympathy vote really.

It was a bit of a shock when Wally hoisted me over his shoulder to chair me off after the game, but it did show one thing about him; when it came to football he had respect for me and as a team-mate he was a good man.

As we waited for the presentations after the game I had my own special little presentation for Wayne Pearce. I had told Junior just before we'd run out not to swap his jersey after the match. When he asked why all I could say was that I had something else planned. After the game I took off my number 13, the international number for lock, and swapped with his number 12 (second-row). He was the heir apparent Australian lock and I simply said to him, "You're going to be wearing this one from now on. Look after it."

Before the series began I had spoken to ARL boss Ken Arthurson about being rested from future representative football. I had to get a letter requesting that I be granted exemption. I felt I had spent enough time away from my family playing representative football—since I had begun playing Union I had spent 12 months all up away on three tours plus the few days at a time for home internationals and a few weeks here and there touring New Zealand. I was 31 and felt I had given my country enough service. Parramatta were paying my bills, but I had missed plenty of club football while playing for NSW and Australia, so I wanted to settle down at home and with Parramatta.

I'd meant for my retirement to become effective as of the end of the season. There was one State of Origin match remaining and Ernie Hammerton, chairman of selectors, asked me to make sure I was available for that final interstate match. I was NSW captain

Farewell Australia

and after losing the first two games, I was dead keen to go out a winner against Queensland.

But I was stabbed in the back. They didn't choose me. I was down in the Snowy Mountains with my Parramatta team-mates, enjoying a few days away after playing Canberra. Stan Jurd told me the NSW side been announced and I wasn't in it. I felt like I'd been booted in the guts.

All sorts of reasons were given: they thought I had retired as from the Test series; they wanted to give Wayne Pearce experience at lock; and they wanted me to go out a winner. That said a lot for the NSW side; the selectors expected them to lose.

As it turned out, Steve Mortimer led the Blues to victory. That I was not there was no misunderstanding, get that straight. It was the selectors' blunder and something I have never forgiven them for.

The Crow and I

WHEN I FIRST met Michael Cronin he reminded me of an altar boy. He had short cropped hair, a pure kid-next-door sort of face, and he was so reserved. I didn't think anything bad could come out of this man's mouth. I watched his character develop during his 10 years at Parramatta and learned he was far from a choir boy, but he always kept the Mr Nice Guy image and was without doubt the most respected footballer in his time.

The Crow came to Parramatta with a big reputation as a goalkicker, much more than as a player. He proved to be a legend at both; that is the one word I would use to describe Michael Cronin. He was one of the greatest goalkickers the game has ever seen, holding just about every point scoring record worth having, but he was just as great as a centre. There have been a lot of fine goalkickers and a lot of fine players, but very few of them can claim to be regarded as greats on both counts.

Michael Cronin was the finest player I played with and I was fortunate never to have played against him. He was also the greatest person I played with. I said on a video made for our testimonial that the best thing was he's just as good out of football boots as he is in them. We have both finished our playing days, but I hope I never lose his friendship.

I still remember his first match for Parramatta in 1977. It was against North Sydney at Cumberland Oval. We won, and Crow scored 17 points from seven goals and a try. I thought then that this guy was more than a goalkicker. He ran, he off-loaded, he picked up a try and he even tackled, although probably the only fault I found with Michael Cronin's game was his defence. Not too many got around him, but he was never renowned for leaving the ground to make a tackle, as I have often reminded him.

A sight that terrorised our opposition and was poetry in motion for Parramatta and its army of supporters. Mick Cronin was the greatest player I had the pleasure of having as a team-mate.

Perpetual Motion

From his first day at Cumberland we went on to strike up a bond between us that I have never shared with another footballer. It was a bond that neither of us realised was so strong, until our last year when we were honoured with a joint testimonial; as the two old blokes of the Parramatta side we drove each other on to finish our careers together.

The parallels in our careers are uncanny. We played 22 Tests each, 16 of them together. We both received Order of Australia medals—I was the first League player to receive one and Mick was the second. We both played in Parramatta's four winning grand finals, we both missed the Eels first midweek cup final victory, in 1980. I hold the record for the most first-grade appearances for Parramatta (259) and the Crow stands equal second on 216 (with Bob O'Reilly). Of course, we both shared a testimonial and we finished our careers on the same day, after the 1986 grand final.

It was very special for me to have the Crow there at the end. And it was probably a bit selfish of me too. I kept on his back to return in 1986 after his career looked to have ended when he was almost blinded in his right eye. I'd always maintained I'd go out on top, when there were no bad memories or loss of form, but with such an injury and after so long out of the game in 1986, I expected Crow to risk those same ambitions.

Naturally he wasn't the player he had been when he came back nearly two thirds into the season, but his presence on the field meant a lot more to Parramatta than outsiders realised.

Michael Cronin always said to me he owed the game more than it owed him. Most of all, he owed Parramatta two goals—for the ones he missed in the 1977 and 1984 grand finals. He repaid his "debt" in the 1986 grand final against Canterbury when we won four points to two, the four points coming from two Cronin goals. It was his final triumph.

That season, however, didn't start so well. In February '86, during a trial against Manly at Cessnock on a Saturday night, Mick almost lost the sight of his eye. I have pretty vivid memories of the night. As usual for me in the first trial, my timing and reflexes were stale and I was cut above the eye after going too low for a tackle and copping a knee. I was being attended to by our trainer Graham Richards when I looked around and saw Crow down getting treatment by Alf Richards. I went back into the play and not long after I noticed a replacement coming on. In trials we ran replacements on and off so it was no big deal, but shortly after

The Crow and I

I looked around and wondered who had been replaced. It took me a while before I realised Crow had gone.

We went into the dressing room at half-time and it all started to hit home. We were told that Crow had been taken straight to hospital with a possible serious eye injury, and, obviously, our first reaction was that he must have been gouged. But our young team-mate Mark Laurie said to coach John Monie, "I think I did it." It wasn't until the next day that we knew the seriousness of it. His career looked like it was finished.

Mark Laurie was shattered when he got to training on Tuesday. By then Monie had looked at the video and confirmed that Laurie's finger had accidently brushed Cronin's eye. I felt so sorry for Pebbles (Laurie). His face showed his feelings. He must have been thinking, "What have I done? I've ended the career of one of the greatest players ever." The players banded together and we worked overtime to get Pebbles's mind off it, to reassure him that no one blamed him, and to give everyone some hope that Michael Cronin might not be finished.

On the Sunday after the game I rang Westmead Hospital, where Crow had been flown by helicopter, to see how he was. They wouldn't tell me anything. As was normal practice, they were giving out information only to family, so I rang a half-hour later and told them I was his brother. I was told that Mick wasn't too good, and that he was going to be in hospital for quite a few days.

It was the Tuesday when I was first allowed to visit him. I don't think my opening line was the right thing to say, but it was a shock to see him looking so bloody awful. "You look terrible, Crow," I told him. He had a green wick coming out of his eye to act as a tear duct so his eye wouldn't water. I could tell he was pretty scared at what might happen to his eye.

"Well you had better pull your finger out," I told him. "I've planned your comeback for our first game of the second round against St George (we had the bye the start of the round). That will give you enough games to beat the Bear's (Bob O'Reilly's) old record of 216 games without the semis included. You can finish second to me.

"And I've got it worked out that we can finish together on grand-final day."

At least I managed to get a smile from him, but I don't think he was anywhere near as confident as I was that he could make it back.

Perpetual Motion

About a month later we had the big first day at the Parramatta Stadium—against St George. Crow was out of hospital and had had his eye patch removed not long before, but his eye looked absolutely dreadful. Hardly anyone knew, not even most of the players, but the club had asked him to officially kick off the main match. I knew this, but Crow told me he didn't want to. It was our day, he wasn't going to be playing, so he'd prefer not to have anyone make a big deal of him. I didn't think he was going to do it.

There was a huge crowd that day and it was one of the most awe-inspiring moments of my career when I walked down the tunnel, leading Parramatta into the stadium we had been waiting for years to have. Peter Sterling was behind me and he got the other players to hang back and let me walk onto the oval a fair way in front of them. The roar from the crowd was just unbelievable; that moment is absolutely irreplaceable. As I looked straight ahead I saw the big lettering that spelled "The Mick Cronin Stand". I felt a bit lonely then without the Crow, but the adrenalin was pumping and the other players ran out all hyped up and all I started to think about was christening the stadium with the biggest game of my life.

Then, after St George ran onto the field, the crowd went absolutely wild and all stood up. There, walking along the halfway mark with the ball, dressed in his club blazer, was Michael Cronin. One of the players said "Hey, the Crow's kicking off", and a shiver went down my spine and probably those of the other blokes as well. The Crow was smiling and mucking around, and he pointed towards Stan Jurd, signalling for him not to drop the ball. When he kicked the ball there was no stopping us. This was our stadium and from that moment it was going to be our competition. Nothing could have lifted us more than having Mick Cronin walk onto the field to be part of the first day at the stadium. The Crow couldn't play, but he was there alright, and it showed in the extra determination we had in everything we did. We beat Saints 36–6 and every player would have got an eight-out-of-10 rating. Peter Sterling played the nearest thing to a perfect game, and got a rare 10-point rating from *Rugby League Week*.

In the next couple of months Crow only came to training occasionally. Every time I saw him I reminded him about when he had to come back. He told me he wanted to, but he virtually couldn't see a thing out of his right eye. It was just one big blur. I was with him a few times when someone came up to him on his right side to get his autograph. He had to turn right around to see who it was.

The Crow and I

He wanted to come back, but he didn't want to make a fool of himself nor let anyone down. He got his brother John to run up and down his local oval at Gerringong (called the Michael Cronin Oval) passing the ball to him from the right side. Then he came out on the paddock at our training and we'd put him on the left wing and passed to him at the end of our backline movements. He still wasn't right for the schedule I set him, but only a few weeks later he declared he was fit to play against Cronulla. He was chosen in reserves and he got through without too many problems, then a fortnight later he was back in firsts against Penrith. And what his presence did for the other players was incredible. He dropped the ball a couple of times, but it wasn't so much because of the eye but more because he tried to get back into the game at the same pace as before. He was a bit rusty. The other backs, like Sterling, Brett Kenny and Steve Ella tried to cover for him, and do him favours, not so much to carry him but more to look after him and repay him for all the looking-after he had done for them over the years. But the Crow didn't want that. He wanted to do it on his own. He couldn't cope with feeling he needed any extra favours. He was happy just to finish a game, kick a few goals and not get in the way, but if he had to have allowances made for him, he would have preferred someone else to have been out there.

People always underestimated Mick Cronin. For starters he was a lot faster than he was given credit for. One day he pulled away from Manly's Russel Gartner, who was recognised as one of the fastest players of the past few years. Crow always preferred to set up a try than score one; when he saw open space he was too busy looking to his left and right for someone to pass to instead of stretching out himself.

He had an incredible calming influence on the younger players and I've never known anyone to have such respect within a football club. I was like the old cranky bugger who drove Parramatta on, and Crow was out there in the backs, a kind of father figure who was always giving the right advice and never got rattled. Even I looked up to Crow with the same kind of respect. He was two years older than me and, as I've said, even as I was playing with him, I saw him as one of the game's legends.

The Crow was a nice guy but at the end he wasn't as quiet as most people thought, nor as innocent. Over the years he came out of his shell a lot. Ray Higgs at first got him going and then Bob O'Reilly continued the transformation. We might have brought him on from an altar boy, but however football at Parramatta changed him, it didn't make him into anything bad, although we did get a bit of aggression into Crow's character at the end. I never thought I'd see him throw a punch, but that happened in 1980 at Lidcombe when he'd had enough of Wests' Ted Goodwin. He was sent off. How's that for irony.

Away from the football pitch the bloke's a dead-set night owl. On tours, when you tend to get out and have a few big nights, most of the players would be ready to crash at midnight or 1 am, but Crow would be just warming up at that stage, looking for someone to kick on with him.

And Crow the night owl was a fascinating person. Parramatta just about always went to the Gold Coast for our end of season trips. Crow slept half the day and came alive at night. He was a legend of end-of-season trips too. At the end of 1985 when we thought he might retire, one of the players got special T-shirts made on the Gold Coast with the words, "Cronin's Last Stand, Gold Coast, 1985".

We got on well with a bloke on the Gold Coast who owned a nightclub called Melbas and often he'd let us have a few free drinks after closing time. One night there were a few of us there, getting into a few drinks on the house and having a really good time. There was a disc jockey playing some great songs and there was a music video screen. We knuckled down to a really good night. Most of the Parramatta players had gone and there was hardly anyone in the joint. The deejay packed up and left, but his equipment was still there so we asked the owner if could we play some music and next thing Brett Kenny and I had turned disc spinners. The Crow and Peter Wynn were merrily chatting away and all was fine. Then, I looked out the window and the sun was up. I rarely have late nights, valuing my sleep too much, so I couldn't believe it. We ended up walking back to our motel, stopping for bacon and eggs at a 24-hour place on the way. The Crow strolled along like it was the normal routine. Brett, Wynnie and I got a few hours sleep before hitting the beach, but Mick slept the whole day, surfacing in time for another social event that night. He could sleep in daylight without any worries. He never liked swimming or the beach, even though he lived on the NSW south coast at Gerringong. He would, however, leave the hotel if there were races on at the Gold Coast. He was a keen punter and the horses started after lunch, which suited him just fine.

My wife Chris and I at Perth Airport with Mick Cronin and his wife Lynn. We were on our way, as guests of the Federal Government, to see the 1987 America's Cup *final between* Kookaburra *and* Stars And Stripes.

Crow helps me limber up before a pre-season training session at Jack Gibson's property near Wauchope, in the midst of the timber industry country of NSW mid-north coast.

Perpetual Motion

Crow always drank Bacardi, never beer, even though he had been pouring beers for years at his family's Gerringong Hotel. Towards the end of his career he acquired a bit of a taste for Kahlua, but normally it was Bacardi.

The terrible twins of our end-of-season trips, Peter Wynn and Paul Mares, tried and tried to get the Crow drunk. They had never seen him drunk, so they always managed to get in a shout with Crow and when they went up to the bar they'd spike his drink. Sometimes they'd come back with triple Bacardis and hardly a drop of Coke in them. Little did they know that Crow was spiking their drinks right back when it was his shout, so invariably Maresy and Wynnie would end up under the table and Crow would keep kicking all night long.

One afternoon they somehow succeeded with their mission. It was the first time I've ever seen the old bloke shot and he was a mess. We had to go for a barbecue that night at Harry Hudson's Gold Coast home, Harry being the boss of Hardies, our sponsors. When we got there Crow passed out, Wynnie also finally collapsed and Maresy was parading around like a kid who had been given a trailbike for Christmas. "I got him, I finally got him. I did it," Maresy was screaming. About half an hour later I noticed Paul Mares curled up on the couch like a baby.

Generally Crow was a model for anyone's son and Parramatta didn't have enough money to pay him what he was worth—as a centre, as a goalkicker and as an example to every player in the club. I often wonder how hard Canterbury secretary Peter Moore kicked himself for knocking him back. Moore had approached Crow about coming to Sydney in 1975. Crow had been playing for Australia from the bush since 1973, and he knocked Moore back, but they struck a deal that if Mick ever went to Sydney it would be with Canterbury. Then right through 1976, Terry Fearnley tried to get Crow to agree to come to Parramatta, but it was months before Crow explained to Terry that he had made a promise to Bullfrog Moore. Terry drove to Bullfrog's office that day to sort it out, and when he learned Canterbury had already signed their 13th import, which was the maximum allowed in those days, Moore allowed Crow to come to Parramatta.

In his first year Crow scored 225 points. In his second year he set a record of 282 points for Sydney first grade. He won the Rothmans Medal both times.

Mick was 25 when he joined the club and no one expected him

The Crow and I

to be there 10 years later, least of all Mick himself. And Michael Cronin's name will live at Parramatta for another lifetime because his name is up there right across the front of one of the grandstands.

I'd be lying if I said I wasn't disappointed at first that my name wasn't on the other stand when the Stadium was opened in 1986. The Sydney Cricket Ground Trust, which runs the ground and organised the naming of the stands and the bars, preferred Ken Thornett's name. I could understand that Mick Cronin holds an incredible amount of records and Thornett, who was known as "The Mayor", really caused the crowds to flock to Cumberland in the early '60s. And I can see the point of having two players from different eras honoured with the naming of each stand. But it would have been special for me to have my name up there along with the Crow's because that's how it was for so much of our careers.

To be honest, I would have been happy for Bob O'Reilly to have been named on the other stand. He was Parramatta's first local junior to play for Australia and was a great mate of Crow's. As it was, the Bear and I each have a bar named after us, which is a great honour. I suppose by having my name across the wall of the bar there is a chance plenty of people will get drunk and eulogise me, so I can't complain.

It's a pity I've got to pay for my drinks in my own bar, though, while Mick Cronin doesn't have to pay for a seat in his own stand. I suppose he was always smarter than me, even if I was better looking.

The Price to Pay

DURING THE 1982 Kangaroo tour I kept a photo album full of family shots beside my bed. I reckon I had quite a bit to do with Telecom's huge profit that year as well; I put in two or three reverse-charge phone calls to Chris each week.

My relationship with my family has been the sad part of my life. My marriage was on thin ice at one stage, mostly through the pressures of football, and I have missed out on half the growing up of my children Ben and Kasey. The hardest thing was that I could see it happening but was helpless to do anything about it.

Mine was a cut-and-dried case of giving football everything or giving it up. I wanted to achieve something and I enjoyed being so competitive, but it was my family that had to make the sacrifices, not me.

I haven't known my children like most fathers. Until I retired I didn't have a normal father–son relationship with Ben. Our big plans now are to go fossicking for a week in the bush; we've never done anything like going camping together. Weekends were always a write-off: training Saturday mornings, a quick dash to see Ben play soccer, doing a little at home with what was left in the day and Saturday night at home because I didn't like to go out a night before a match.

My children have never known me either. But Chris does. In fact she is the only person in the world who really knows me. She knows my moods, what drives me, what annoys me, my good habits and my bad habits. It was heartwrenching to have to push her away so often, but it was what I had to do if I wanted to succeed as a footballer.

I suppose it is hard for people who have never been in the situation to understand. The person best equipped to talk about

The Price to Pay

the family life, or lack of it, for a footballer is Chris herself. Here is her story.

The hardest thing about being the wife of a famous footballer is the loneliness. Your husband is rarely ever there. You find yourself being both mother and father to your children. Then, on top of that, you have to accept the loss of your identity. Your individuality disappears. You are acknowledged as nothing but "his missus" and most times you feel like you should be walking 10 metres back behind your man.

I am very proud of Ray Price the footballer. His success opened doors for us and has given us things in life we would have only dreamed of, but there is another side of fame. It's the price you pay. I'm sure most people would sit back and think, "Oh, they have a lovely house and it must be so fantastic to be well known." I would like to set them straight, and I'm sure mine is a story many wives of leading sportsmen can identify with.

We have two children who for all their lives have had a part-time father. Having a leading footballer as a dad puts an incredible pressure on a family. Our marriage felt the weight of that pressure for its first 11 years, while Raymond played football.

There was a time when I was going to pack up and leave. I didn't marry Raymond so we could lead separate lives. I could have had kids without getting married. Sometimes I thought I would have coped better like that; knowing that without a husband, and accepting that from the start, I would have managed by myself. I thought having a part-time husband and father was worse than not having anyone at all.

My mother convinced me otherwise. If it wasn't for her I would have left and never come back. The matter blew up before Raymond left for the 1982 Kangaroo tour. He was selected and had decided without consulting me that he was going away again for three months. I felt I couldn't take that anymore, and decided to leave; we had spoken about it many times. I thought it was about time my life started rather than me being the one who just stayed home and waited.

Mum sat me down and talked to me. Ray, too, confided in her, as he had often done. I told mum I couldn't stand having Ray part-time anymore, but she pointed out that a part-time father and husband was better than none, and that the children needed someone living in the house whom they called dad. It would have been too much an interruption in their lives to pack up and leave.

At that point I decided that when Raymond returned from the Kangaroo tour it would be my turn to sample a bit of life. I started going out with my girlfriends and going to bingo with my mum. I started to renew old friendships. On Saturday nights I went out and did some of the things I had missed out on. I loved dancing (Ray hated to dance), so I went out to discos with my girlfriends. It also gave Raymond a chance to be at home with the kids so that if something went wrong he was the one they called for. My life began to fit into Ray's spare time and that went on for about 18 months before I started to realise the children had had a part-time father for too long and didn't need a part-time mother as well.

Our marriage then settled down again and we gradually got back together closer than before.

Rugby League at the top can affect you in so many ways. When we started going out Raymond was playing Rugby Union; we had been engaged for only four months when he went away for four months on the Wallaby tour. Then he switched to League, but we had no idea what that was going to mean. We had no idea how good Ray was going to be at League, or how much he was about to achieve, or how much pressure we could continually be under. Sitting at home waiting for those first four months to pass was hell, but generally that is all I have done since.

There was more than just two or three nights training and a game on Sunday. There were promotions and trips away for representative football. On an average he was home two nights a week during the football season for 11 years. Raymond always had to keep the club, the sponsors and the fans happy—but not the family. Football was first, his job was second, we always came third.

Ray Price the footballer was hard and dedicated. He could achieve anything he put his mind to. He ate and slept football, and that was all that mattered to him.

But Raymond Price the husband and father. He can be a cold-hearted person, often without realising. He is honest and always says exactly what he feels without stopping to think of how it might hurt people's feelings. On the other hand, he can be a really humorous person, always joking. He is a friendly person, but if he doesn't like someone he will let them know. Deep down he is a shy person, believe it or not, although he has never lacked confidence.

The Price to Pay

The difference between the two Ray Prices was never more evident than when he arrived at the ground on a Sunday. As soon as he entered the gate he became Ray Price the footballer, as if a hypnotist had just snapped his fingers. If he was stopped to sign autographs, I'd always say "Goodbye, have a good game". I'm not sure if it meant anything to him. In an instant he had switched off; I could have been on the sideline or at home watching television and it wouldn't have mattered to him. What really mattered was that he went out and played his best to win. He'd shut himself off to everything outside that. When I saw him again after a game, he had cooled down and become Raymond Price again.

I knew he hated losing, but he was never a bad loser in my eyes. Often one of his team-mates would come out of the dressing room first and say "Gee, I pity you tonight. He's in a rotten mood." But I can honestly say he never came home bad tempered. He'd be quiet for a while, but that was all. I suppose it fitted with his two separate characters; he became a different person when he was away from the ground.

The media always painted an image of Raymond as the dedicated family man: the one who always went straight home after training to his wife and kids and left the club early after the game. What a load of crap! How could he be a dedicated family man when football took up almost his entire life? Sure, Raymond used to come straight home from training because he couldn't see the sense in training his guts out then going and filling his belly full of beer. And he was always mindful that he had to get up early for work. He has always been an early starter. He is a sort of person who would do almost anything for me, if it didn't interfere with you-know-what. He can show his love for me yet he finds it difficult to show his love for his children by cuddling them or showing outward affection. Maybe it's because he had never learned how during his own childhood.

And I didn't make a big deal over Ray nor did I pamper him. One player's wife I recall was a real mollycoddler, though, and her husband lapped it all up. The pressure she put on him was amazing. She'd treat him like a sook; he only had to prick a finger and she'd have him out of action for two weeks. He missed plenty of games, too.

People wonder what it was like to tend Ray's many injuries. He has always been thought of as the kind of player who slept with an ice-bag all night. Raymond always worked very hard on his

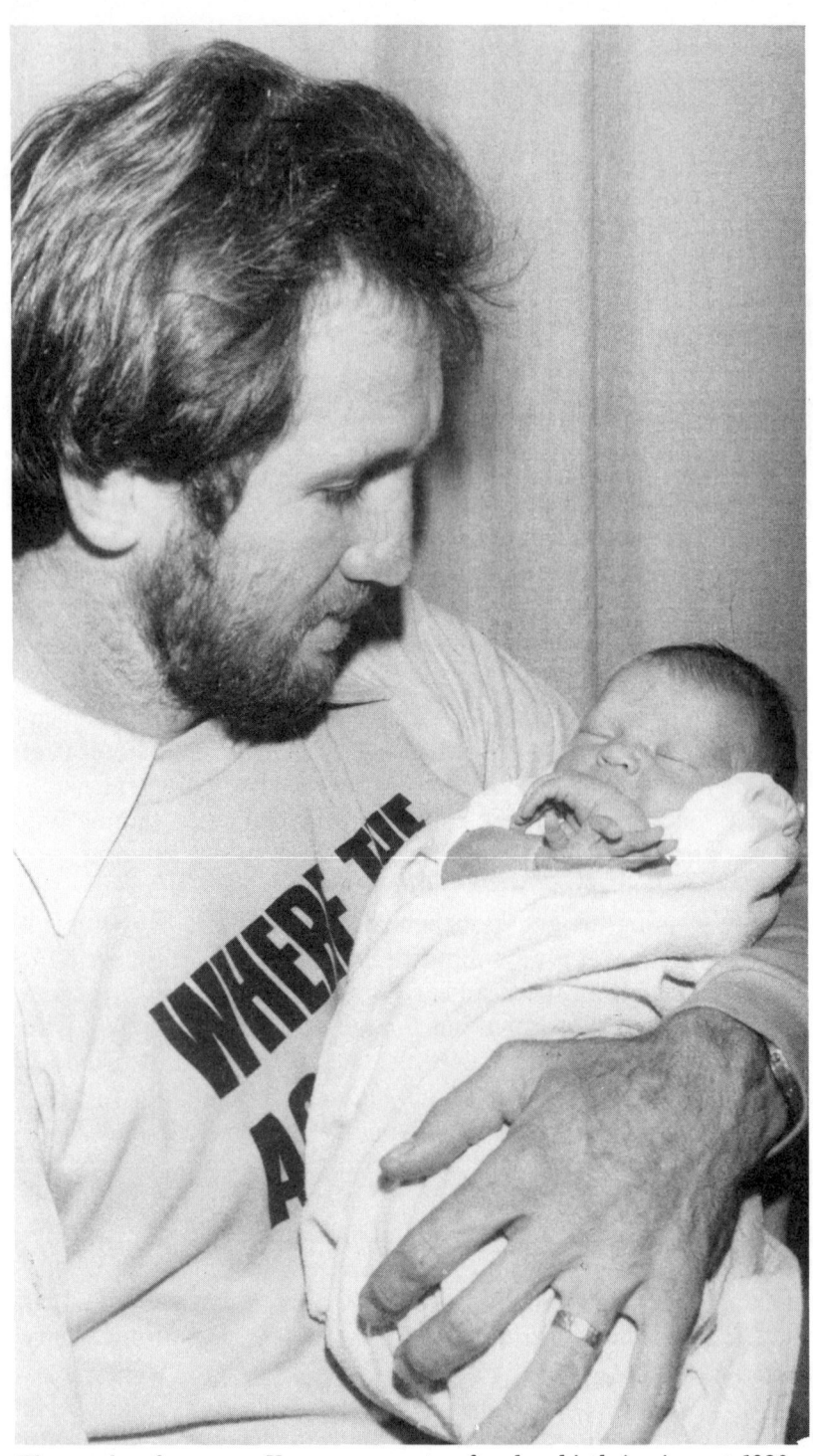

The apple of my eye, Kasey, moments after her birth in August 1980.

The Price family outside a great little cafe not far from home in the western Sydney suburb, Georges Hall.

Surviving a Sydney heatwave with my kids, Ben and Kasey.

injuries, but apart from the first couple of seasons, we never shared our double bed with an ice-bag. At first I thought that to deal with his injuries I would have to dote on him and run around after him, but that was long ago. He did his dash back in 1981 after Parramatta's first grand-final win. After a big night at the club, Raymond had not done any work on his injured knee, and when we got home his knee locked up. I had to carry him out of the car and inside. Next day I had to drive him down to the doctor's and then it was off for x-rays at the hospital. I had to virtually spoon-feed the poor darling, he was so crook. Then on the way home from Parramatta we were driving past Grumpy's pub (the Albion Hotel) when Ray piped up. "Just drop me off here," he said. Suddenly he was well enough to go drinking with the boys. I kicked him out, screamed at him and told him that was the last time I was running around after him when he was hurt. As it turned out, a drink at Grumpy's the day after a grand final became a bit of a ritual.

Raymond was a bit of a sook when it came to his aches and pains. At the club after a match he would be perfect, no worries, but often he'd walk in the door at home and say, "Aw, it hurts", or "Gee my shoulder is sore". He'd expect me to run around and get an ice-bag and a nice hot drink. In the end my attitude was a bit like the proverbial Iron Lady's. I thought, "If you play the game, you take the injuries with it. There's no use coming home and whingeing about it."

Before a match Raymond was like a hyperactive kid. He'd wake up in the morning and the energy was bubbling out of him. He was a tormenting so-and-so who would never shut up and couldn't keep still. When the kids were little he used to get the stuffed toys and throw them around the room and wrestle with them. And when Ben got bigger he used to wrestle with him. Ben loved it. But once Ray got to the game, things became serious.

Ben and Kasey are the ones who have suffered the most from football, particularly Ben. We live in the Canterbury district at Bass Hill and because of that there has been a lot of trouble for Ben at school. Other kids tormented him because he was Ray Price's son. Canterbury and Parramatta have become arch enemies in recent years and that applied to the playground too, I can assure you, especially around grand-final time.

We have had to take Ben off the school bus a few times because he had been bashed up by other kids. One day he had come home

The Price to Pay

from school on the bus, but we couldn't find him. We looked everywhere and eventually found him hiding in our wardrobe crying his eyes out. At least there he thought he was safe from the kids calling him names and tormenting him.

Benjamin hates being the son of Ray Price the footballer. He's accused of thinking he's smart simply because he is Ray's son. He is a very shy boy who lacks confidence, which is not surprising. He plays soccer and I hope he never plays League because of the pressure that will be on him. He's got it now and he doesn't even play the game. Ben hates getting his photo in the paper with Ray because he gets embarrassed and stirred at school.

Kasey doesn't go through nearly as much, and is still a bit young to understand. And being a girl she doesn't get hassled as much. Occasionally she gets, "You're Ray Price's daughter". All she says back is "So what!"

They suffered most by not having Raymond home. Ray and Ben didn't have a father-son relationship because of it. Ben couldn't talk to his dad because he became accustomed to telling me his troubles and sharing his joys, but since Ray has retired Ben has come out of his shell a hell of a lot and their relationship has improved a great deal. They are both enjoying that chance.

There was one time, with Ben just a baby, when Ray felt another dimension of the strain of being a high-profile footballer as well as a father. Benjamin was a very sickly baby, with colic and reflux; he didn't have a full night's sleep until he was four years old. When he came home from hospital, not long after he was born in 1978, he was screaming all the time. Raymond and I did hourly shifts, one of us at a time, walking up and down the hall nursing him. That went on for almost six months.

At that time a few critics were on Raymond's back about a supposed form slump. It wasn't as if he was playing badly, it was just that he wasn't as outstanding as they had come to expect. They never knew why. He was under a lot of pressure. In the end my mum stopped us from going insane; she came over and watched Ben for us quite often, and my dad did the same quite often too. Ray has always been thankful for that—and I have been too.

Another side of sporting fame is being interrupted when you go out in public. Ray accepts that his face is well known and people will always come up to him. He has always said the fans are the most important part of the game. I can understand that, and at first, when Ray started to become well known, I got a bit of a kick out of it. But over 11 years it has pushed the privacy out of our lives.

When people walk past and say "Gooday Ray", that's just natural. When people come up and are rude and ignorant, with me standing next to him like a faceless shadow, it becomes a little overbearing. People think they might be the first ones to come up and rave on, but next thing it takes three hours to walk from one end of a shopping centre to the other.

It's worse in restaurants. People don't come up and politely interrupt while we are looking at the menu or waiting for our first course to arrive. No, they wait until you are about to take your first mouthful of food, then appear suddenly from nowhere, shove between you, hold out a bit of paper and say, "I know I'm annoying you, but...." I practically bite my lip. I would certainly hate to be married to a movie star who is known all around the world and always getting mobbed. You just couldn't be yourself. People are always checking out what you are wearing. It's as if you couldn't pick your nose without being spotted. I've always waited for that big headline in the papers: "Ray Price Picks Nose".

Wives in Rugby League have never really had a great time. Neither the clubs or the League have worked overtime to make wives feel part of football's society, but things are getting better. For years we had to find our own seats like everyone else at the football, even on grand-final day. Then we got tickets for the big day of the year, but no guaranteed seat. In 1984 the League even allocated seats for us—right along the fence in front of the Noble Stand, beside the Canterbury wives. The view was okay when there wasn't a big truck loaded with sound equipment in front of us. In 1986 we were allowed into the members area and for the first time someone from Parramatta made sure we were comfortable and showed us to seats that had been kept aside for us. We were even allowed in the ante-room off the main dressing room after Parramatta had won. We appreciated that.

In earlier years we sat wherever we could. One day at Brookvale Oval, Ray's sister Marilyn and I had to sit on the hill, and some Manly fans were giving Ray heaps, calling him "Cement Head" and plenty of things worse. Unable to take any more, we had a go back at them, and all of a sudden some girls started coming at us. If a man sitting next to us hadn't warded them off we would have been dead meat. We certainly learned from that day that it was best to keep our mouths shut.

Chris and I at the Dally M awards in 1982, with Mick Cronin, Steve Ella, and Jack Gibson. Chris loved to go to such functions, but there were too few where wives were welcomed.

Signing autographs soon after arriving at a ground for a match was the point Chris reckoned I turned from Ray Price, husband, to Ray Price, footballer.

Perpetual Motion

Since 1986, Parramatta wives have been allocated home-game seats at the front of the Ken Thornett Stand—rows A and B. They sound like the best seats in the house don't they? No way. In row A you couldn't see because of a rail across the front of the stand, and in row B you could see alright—if you stretched your neck. It stuck in my throat when I turned around to see all the committeemen, their wives and kids, sitting comfortably up the back with a great view.

Raymond and Michael Cronin became life members of the Parramatta club, which meant they were each given two seats at the back of the stand. Lyn Cronin and I often sat there, but I thought other wives had their noses out of joint. I think I was then seen as a snob, and that didn't help. My feeling was that we all should have been given good seats; it shouldn't have needed life membership. I went to watch the football which wasn't the case with all wives. I'd had nothing to do with football before I met Raymond, but I grew to love it and thought it was my role to be there lending him support.

Naturally I got to know a lot of the player's wives and girlfriends well. Over the years I made a lot of acquaintances, but only one really good friend, Julie Kenny. There were others I became reasonably close to, such as Lyn Cronin, Lynne Hilditch and Julie Monie.

To me, a friend is someone I can confide in, tell my troubles to, show off my things to. We all got on rather well, but I admit I felt uneasy whenever I mentioned that we had just bought something new, or if Ray had won an award, which usually yielded an appliance like a video or dishwasher. I felt they were probably thinking, "Here she goes, bragging again". I wasn't. Football has given us many things we wouldn't have otherwise had and I didn't see anything wrong in wanting to tell my friends about it. I've always liked good jewellery. I was never able to have anything like that when I was younger and it was a big thrill to have something really nice. Sometimes I felt I was despised for it.

To set the record straight about the "other" side of fame might sound like me ridding myself of 11 years of frustration, but there were some good things I enjoyed about being a Rugby League widow. There were great moments too and a lot of positive things about Ray's success, and there were many times when I was very, very proud of him. To be beside him sometimes made me feel as if I was up there on a pedestal as well. He was one of the game's

The Price to Pay

greats. There were plenty of good footballers around, but Raymond was a great footballer, and not too many can achieve that kind of standing in the game.

Watching him hold up the National Panasonic Cup in 1986 was a moving moment. I knew how much he wanted it because he had been injured the only time Parramatta had won it before in 1980. At Ray and Mick Cronin's testimonial dinner, in 1986, everyone stood up and applauded, clearing an aisle for us as we walked into the Parramatta Leagues Club auditorium. There aren't words to describe that atmosphere. And when we were sitting there watching a film about Ray's and Mick's careers, I just wanted to cry. I was ill that night and ended up in hospital a few days later with pneumonia, but I wouldn't have missed that night for the world.

Winning the *Daily Mirror*'s best-and-fairest award, the Dally M gold medal in 1982, was such a proud moment too, and it was one of the few functions where women were invited, and I could be there to savour Ray's experience with him. When he won the prestigious Rothman's Medal, for being best-and-fairest player of 1979 as voted by the referees, it was also marvellous, but the elation was spoiled because the awards night was a men only affair. Being presented with the Caltex NSW Sports Star Award was possibly even more important because it had judged people from all sports, but that occasion was soured by a big back-page photo in the next day's newspaper of a female trotting driver giving Ray a congratulatory kiss. I felt it should have been me, his wife, kissing him, but again I was at home, uninvited; again pushed aside, so unimportant. Just his missus.

One of the most vivid memories was that final moment, when Parramatta won the 1986 grand final and we knew it was to be Raymond's last game. It was a fairytale ending for him. As soon as the hooter sounded I looked for him. I found myself crying, and I looked at Ben—it was the first time we had taken him to a grand final—and he was starting to cry too. He knew his father had done what he had wanted to, and Ben realised dad was going to be home now. There was to be no more football.

My Canterbury Hate

STRANGE AS IT MAY seem with all my Parramatta connections, I have lived in the Canterbury district for the past seven years, in the Bass Hill and Georges Hall area. A lot of people, even children, have been very spiteful towards my family. The day my son Ben came home from school petrified and hid in the wardrobe after he had been bullied on the bus by other kids, because he was my son, will live in my memory forever.

At semi-final time we couldn't let Ben travel on the bus because of the treatment he was getting. Chris had to drive him to and from school. When he was in first class, just six years old, a couple of second-year boys bashed him up because they hated Parramatta. Ben didn't understand. He knew I played football, but he had rarely been to a match and knew nothing about the rivalry between Parramatta and Canterbury.

The torture my kids had to go through was the main reason behind what some people saw as my private war against the Bulldogs. I have to admit I developed a hate for Canterbury towards the end of my career. It wasn't so much a dislike of the team's players, but more a dislike of the name Canterbury, because it had meant a lot of pain for my family.

As well as that, I have not been impressed with the style of football Canterbury have played since Warren Ryan took over as coach. The Bulldogs used to be the "entertainers", the best in the business when it came to open, spontaneous football. Fair enough, under Ryan they have won two premierships up to 1986, but they have became a dead, dull team which has relied on antagonising and intimidating their opposition.

I can't say I enjoyed playing Canterbury, and that had nothing to do with them being a side which could often beat us. There is

My Canterbury Hate

too much needling in their game, unnecessary stuff which has only surfaced since Ryan joined the club in 1984.

I don't know what sort of bloke Warren Ryan is, other than he seems pretty volatile and arrogant, and wherever he goes controversy seems to follow.

The style of football he has introduced at Canterbury works. He brought them successive premierships in 1984 and 1985, but the 1985 grand-final win against St George (7-6) was boring. They intimidated St George, pinned them in their own territory with bombs and, as Canterbury always do in their big matches, concentrated on putting key players out of the match. St George centre Michael O'Connor was fouled early in the match, Graeme Wynn was king-hit after his sensational start to the game. It was not my type of football even though people claim I was pretty aggressive myself. Only one try was scored by each team in that grand final, the same as the year before when the Bulldogs beat Parramatta 6-4. And in 1986 there were no tries scored when we beat Canterbury 4-2. That's the type of game the Bulldogs play in the big ones.

There's no question, Canterbury was a great side. In the first six years of the 1980s Parramatta won four premierships and Canterbury won two. From 1984 Canterbury was as good as Parramatta; the difference boiled down to who played better on the day. We had knocked them out of the finals in 1983 and they knocked us out in 1984 (grand final) and 1985, when they beat us 26-0 in the final, then we knocked them out in the 1986 grand final. But Canterbury would be much more respected if they played with the same amount of intensity and took all the crap out of their game.

The classic example of Ryan's influence is Terry Lamb. Lamb was a great competitor when he was at Wests; even then he was the best backer-up in the game and he used to score tries with his own individual brilliance as well. He was tough, and there was no mug in him, but when he went to Canterbury a deal of sledging and bitchiness crept into his game. It was as if he took angry pills before a match. One time I saw him run 30 metres to sledge an opposing player who had made a mistake. He may have become more aggressive because he had an aggressive pack in front of him, but I think there was more to it than that. I don't know what he was trying to prove.

Paul Langmack is a player who would have no bounds if he took the silliness out of his play. I've always regarded Langmack as a great lock and an exceptional player. He was a Parramatta junior and we thought he would play for Parramatta before Canterbury secretary Peter Moore snuck in and offered him a few dollars to go to the Bulldogs when he was only 17. He probably did the right thing because he got more opportunity at Canterbury—there was no way I was going to give him the number eight jersey at Parramatta.

Langmack's mouth gets him into trouble. He has always liked to sledge and carry on, but in 1986 he became too costly for his team by giving away too many penalties. He doesn't need that stuff and he has to realise it just like I did. I don't think Paul even realises how good he could be.

The Bulldogs have had a great leader in Steve (Turvey) Mortimer. There are some things Turvey has said and done which I don't agree with, but I have a huge respect for him as a player, and he has proved to be one of the great captains of the game with NSW and Canterbury.

When I rate players I always consider firstly their workrate. I like a player who is at it for the whole 80 minutes, because to me, that is the real mark of a good player. With that in mind, I regard Peter Sterling as a better halfback than Steve Mortimer. They play different games. Sterlo is an organiser, a great tactical kicker who makes a lot of tackles on the front line. Mortimer plays in fits and starts. He is also a good tactical kicker, a magnificent cover defender and, when he gets into the game, he is electrifying with the ball. You can't afford to hang off Turvey because if you give him half an opening he is through for a try.

Talk about giving someone at Canterbury half an opening always raises the spectre of Mark Bugden and the try he scored to win the 1984 grand final, while I lay on the ground injured. I've copped the blame for that try, but my conscience is clear. I don't blame myself. I had tackled Steve Mortimer a few seconds earlier and thought I had snapped my arm. I went back into the play but my arm had gone numb from my wrist to my elbow. I went into another tackle and just couldn't feel anything, so I went down waiting for attention. That's when Mark Bugden noticed me and took off down the blind side from dummy-half. I wouldn't have been able to tackle him if I was in the line, and one person out of the line shouldn't have enabled the dummy-half to sprint 20 metres to score. Bugden beat two tacklers, John Muggleton, who shouldn't have missed him, and then Paul Taylor. To me it was a

I developed a hatred for Canterbury, not because of the players but the name and the heartache it caused my family.

Oh to be young again, and to be able to step out like I did in the early days with the Eels.

My Canterbury Hate

case of credit being given when it was due. Mark Bugden read the play well and showed a lot of determination to score what proved the match winning try.

We had the stuffing knocked out of us that day when we lost centre Steve Ella with a serious knee injury early in the match. Canterbury had targeted Ella and Brett Kenny and tried to take them out of the game. They didn't expect to get Ella off the field and there wasn't any suggestion of illegality in the tackle that busted him, but we knew darn well that Ella and Kenny were Canterbury's targets to be intimidated enough to put them off their game.

David Liddiard came on to replace Ella and played quite well. Late in the game he made a break and only a bad pass which was intercepted by Canterbury winger Steve O'Brien cost us a draw or a win. The following season Liddiard ended up the villain again when he dropped a bomb in the final that led to a Canterbury try to winger Matthew Callinan just after half-time. We were behind only 4-0 at the break but that blunder broke our backs. Too many Parramatta players obviously thought we were beaten at that stage and we went on to get thrashed 26-0.

It was a sour end to what had been a courageous 1985 season for Parramatta. We had played the first two months without Brett Kenny, Peter Sterling, Eric Grothe, Neil Hunt, John Muggleton and Paul Taylor, who had all decided to play club football in England.

We played terribly in the first match going down 26-6 against St George, but after that the "second stringers" banded together to develop a fantastic team spirit. It was my first season away from representative football and I had been looking forward to devoting all my energies to Parramatta. With Michael Cronin, Steve Ella, Peter Wynn and Graeme Atkins, who had returned from Easts, providing the experience, we were in third position when all the stars returned home. Players like Liddiard, Matt Carter, Greg Henry, Mike Eden, Tony Chalmers, Steve Broughton, Gary Phillips, Peter Ford, Glenn Mansfield and Vince Carr were hardly household names at Parramatta but they really did their jobs. We were able to keep the side together with Geoff Bugden, Steve Sharp, Stan Jurd and Paul Mares also contributing a lot, and we really gathered some momentum. The attitude was that when the stars returned from England they had to earn their spots.

However, when the more recognised players returned, we seemed to lose steam. Then Peter Sterling, Brett Kenny and Paul Mares were hit with injuries and representative football took more players away from us. That year was the first time we were beaten by Canberra. It was the day after a Test match and we had fielded Paul Taylor, Neil Hunt, Michael Cronin, Mark Laurie, Tony Chalmers, Ron Quinn, Mike Eden, myself, Peter Ford, Steve Sharp, Glenn Mansfield, Vince Carr, and Stan Jurd.

When the representative football had finished we started to show some form and then ran hot for the first two weeks of the semi-finals. We thrashed Penrith 38-6 first up, but the Panthers had to go through a play-off for fifth spot against Manly during the week before that game and seemed as if they had played their big match after celebrating making the semi-finals for the first time. We then beat Balmain again, by 32-4, after flogging them 40-8 in the second round. In 1986 we continued our superiority over the Tigers with scores of 23-8, 32-4 and 32-16 (Panasonic Cup final). I don't think we had built up any psychological hoodoo over Balmain, I just think we had been lucky with dream starts to practically every match, scoring a try in the opening minutes. Balmain were a young side then which has since been nurtured over quite a few years into a more mature team. They have always been an inconsistent side, and whenever we got a roll on against them they didn't know how to handle us.

People have said that if any team could ever win the premiership from fourth or fifth spot it was Parramatta that season. When we didn't, they claimed it would never be done. I don't agree. The key to doing it from fourth or fifth is your injury toll. If you can keep the same side intact it is quite possible to go all the way. Winning breeds confidence and when you come up against a side that has had a week's break, or two if they were the minor premiers who had won the major semi-final, a team that has momentum and no injuries will knock off the favourites. The greatest example of how a side can storm home from the bottom half of the semi-finals was South's incredible effort in 1955 when they won 11 straight matches to win the premiership.

A team will win the premiership from fourth or fifth spot before the 1980s are over. Our nemesis, Canterbury, ended our hopes of me proving that point. They were too good on the day in 1985.

They beat us again in the first round of 1986, but from then Parramatta won the next five straight against the Bulldogs including a Panasonic Cup match in 1986, which disproved the theory that our forwards weren't tough enough to handle them. We didn't have to resort to sledging to do it although it disappointed me that we did retaliate with that sort of business in that first round match at Parramatta Stadium in 1986.

At least I had the guts to say what most people were thinking when I called Canterbury sledgers and whingers in my *Rugby League Week* column after we had beaten them in a National Panasonic Cup match. I'd really had a gutful of how they were carrying on and thought I'd get it off my chest after we had beaten them, not lost to them so people could not claim I was suffering a case of sour grapes.

My column was posted to every player in the Canterbury club by the Bulldog secretary Peter Moore and apparently it was used as a big psyche up for the premiership match against us a few weeks later. If they needed that sort of motivation they'd have to be kidding, and if they reckoned my column had something to do with our defeat, that's just as much hogwash. If they were so fired up about my comments before the game why were we leading them at half-time? We lost because we made some costly mistakes which Canterbury capitalised on. That was all that won them the match.

The Canterbury players carried on like spacemen again and in the second half a brawl broke out after an altercation. The thing that disappointed me most was that some of our players retaliated with their own sledging, which was something we didn't need and only showed that we were being intimidated.

Canterbury have developed such a siege mentality under Warren Ryan that they like to think the world hates them. If they have intimidated you, they feel they have carried out their job. It will be interesting to see how Canterbury play the game when Warren Ryan is gone.

The Sometimes Philosopher

IN MY 11 SEASONS with Parramatta I didn't receive one offer from another Sydney club. That may come as a surprise, but it's true. Apparently there were a couple of feelers but they didn't reach my ears, going only as far as my manager John White.

There were two reasons. One was that I didn't want to play for anyone else but Parramatta and the other was that I had always agreed to a new contract long before my existing contract expired. I signed four agreements with the Eels. The first three were for three years each and the last one was for only two because I had expected that that would see me to the end of my career.

I may have been criticised for many things during my career and I have definitely trodden on a lot of toes and found myself in trouble after making comments without sometimes stopping to think of the consequences, but two things I always believed in were honesty and loyalty. When it came to playing for Parramatta, I was honest with myself and I knew I could never be happy with another club. The loyalty followed naturally.

Loyalty was a very big thing at Parramatta in the 1980s. David Liddiard was the only top player Parramatta wanted to keep who left. He went to Penrith in 1986. I'd like to think I had a fair bit to do with all our internationals staying.

There was a stage at the end of 1985 when there were big offers for Peter Sterling, Steve Ella, Brett Kenny and Eric Grothe, and I thought we could have lost them. I turned into a politician for a couple of weeks and did everything, including threatening them in the end, to ensure they stayed at Parramatta. I was on the phone to them and went around to their places, pointing out all the benefits of staying for the sake of a few less dollars. I told them they had been happy and established at Parramatta and that mightn't be the case if they changed clubs; there would be no guarantee they would fit into the style of play at another club, it would always be further to travel. There was a sense of belonging and confidence at Parramatta, built from years of sticking together. I didn't want to see that go. After I discussed with them all the pros and cons of leaving, I left them with one thought: "If you do go, I'm going to make it so unbearable when you play against me, you'd wish you'd never made the move." I don't think that had much to do with them all staying, but I suppose it showed them how serious I was about what I was saying to them.

When we went four years without a home ground, Parramatta did suffer quite a bit in the hip pocket. All our top players could have picked up probably $10,000 to $20,000 a season more at some of the wealthier clubs. I know Manly offered Brett Kenny the world to go there, but money isn't everything in Rugby League and the players knew that when the Parramatta Stadium was built things would work out financially better for them in the long run.

I know I've got a reputation for being "tight" with my cash, but I have never played football for the money. I played Rugby Union for many years for no money at all. Parramatta looked after me well in my last few seasons but I doubt that I was anywhere near the best paid player in the game. Money was important, sure, and I always tried to do the best financially for myself and my family. Players chopped and changed clubs like never before in the late '70s and early '80s, and there were some clubs, like Easts and Manly, who had plenty of high-priced players but didn't have the spirit. You can't put a price on spirit and loyalty. Parramatta picked up four premierships from those qualities and I reckon they are just about the richest rewards you could ask for.

I did however receive some hefty offers to play in England during my last couple of seasons, but again I wasn't interested. I'm still not aware of some of the offers because my manager John White probably never told me. He knew it was something I would have liked to have done when I was single and younger, but I don't think it would have been a good idea to cart my family over there in the cold and expect the kids to change schools for eight months so I could play football. I had to start thinking about setting myself up in business for my life after football and going to England for the best part of a year wouldn't have helped. I dearly would have loved to have played at Wembley because it's an ambition of every footballer, but I won't lose any sleep over not having that experience.

Parramatta is a great League club and I am proud that in Rugby Union and Rugby League I have only worn the Parramatta jersey. I would be lying if I said I have always agreed with how the Club was run, and I have had some ding-dong battles with secretary Denis Fitzgerald over the years, particularly in the last three seasons when I was captain. The confrontations were always over the same subject: players' rights.

Fitzy probably hated my guts in the end, I'm sure of that, but he was very professional and he overlooked his dislike for me to conduct things in a businesslike manner. I certainly never disliked Fitzy; we argued on matters of principle. I didn't mind a good old argument, and Fitzy and I had plenty, but in our own ways we were trying to achieve the same thing and that was what was best for the club.

I became angry with him over a few things. When he first became secretary in 1979 he was seen as a players' man, but he changed over the years. Without a home ground and the Parramatta Leagues Club not performing all that well for quite some years, making money seemed more important than making the players happy. I got a bee in my bonnet over that; it never seemed as if the club considered the players to be the most important thing. As far as I am concerned, people went to see the players play, not to watch the League Club grow or the directors doing their stuff.

Our most frequent arguments were over sponsors' dinners. I had always maintained that players' wives should have been invited, but I was told the sponsors wouldn't have wanted that and it would have cost too much money. Fitzy's point in the end was that there was even a restriction on how many people each sponsor could bring. But I was pretty stubborn on that case and I wouldn't bend.

The game doesn't do enough for players' families. If a player's wife and kids are happy, the player is happy. If he can go to a game and not have to worry about finding his wife something as simple as a good seat, he can concentrate on his game and not waste any time.

Compared to most administrators in the game, however, Denis Fitzgerald is one of the very best. I have never doubted his honesty or his intentions and he's very professional in how he conducts himself. Indirectly, he inspired me to keep performing for so long at the top level. I was told by someone else, shortly after Fitzy became secretary, that he reckoned I wouldn't last more than a couple more seasons, so as long as Parramatta kept offering me a new contract, the more I thought I had proved a point to Denis Fitzgerald.

Maybe I was hard to get on with. It's difficult for me to say. I've always spoken my mind and I don't back down if I think I am right. It's not in my nature to retreat, nor hoist the white flag. I am very emphatic on a lot of subjects; there is no grey with me, just black and white.

And possibly the clearest of all my opinions over the years are my views on drugs in sport. I never have and never would have taken drugs to get me on the paddock. In my earlier years quite a few players at Parramatta and other clubs took "uppers". I don't know if they were actually amphetamines or not. They thought the pills helped them, but I think it was more a psychological boost than physical. It was all in their minds. It showed a weakness of character.

If you can't get through on your own guts, power and willpower, then it's not worth doing. Players who take little "helpers" are nothing but plastic heroes for the thousands of people who watch them. I wouldn't even take painkillers. If I couldn't get onto the paddock naturally, I wouldn't play.

I knew Graham (Shovels) Olling took steroids to build him up in size when he was at Parramatta. I certainly wouldn't do it, but I could understand Shovels wanting to and he did take the drugs under strict guidance. Nobody knew he was taking them until it came out publicly; obviously it was not something he was going to volunteer to his team-mates. But he never tried to hide it from us once we knew.

I could have done with an extra few pounds myself and in fact I tried a weight program at the end of the 1979 season under a guy called George Chappell. I was only about 86 kg (13½ stone) and he put me on a special diet coupled with a weight-lifting course which included a lot of speed work, repetitions and dead lifts. I went up to around 89 kg (14 stone), but I became a bit cumbersome and during summer most of it fell off me. I realised I wasn't made to carry weight and in the end I played about 86 kg for about my last six seasons.

This all revolves around an attitude about sport that I've held pretty strongly over the years, and that is that if you look after

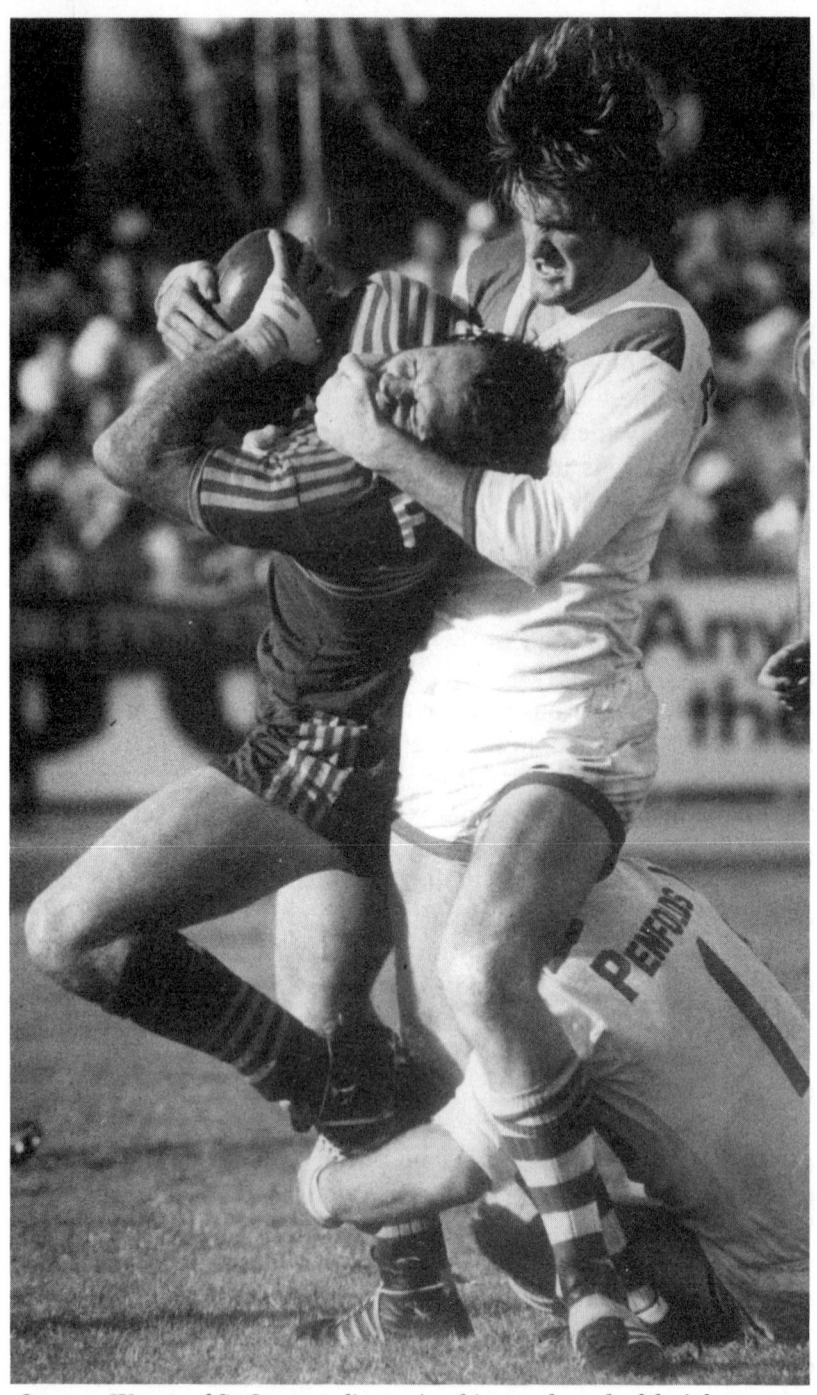

Graeme Wynn, of St George, dispensing his own brand of facial massage. His brother Peter played with me at Parramatta, but injuries marred his career.

Eels trainer Graham Richards steadies me after I had gone down from a blow to my head. Though many people thought I had an inclination to take a swan dive or two, I also copped a few beauties to the head in my final years.

Alf Richards, Parramatta and Australian medico during much of my career, coaxes me to my feet after I had received a knock.

your body it will look after you in return. Sure, you can't avoid serious injuries like knee ligaments and broken bones, but I have always been puzzled by players missing games with common injuries like a corked thigh or simple bruising. Most times such players haven't treated their injuries early enough or well enough.

A footballer is like a carpenter; if his tools aren't sharp he won't do a good job. If I had a cork, I wouldn't spend all night at the club, then home to bed and worry about treatment in the morning only to find I couldn't walk. I would get the ice to it straight away and stay up to all hours with ice on it if I had to.

I always believed in going to work on Mondays because it helped work out my injuries, and I would always train on Tuesday nights, again to help work out my sore spots. I knew many players over the years who would look for any excuse not to train on Tuesday, supposedly because they were carrying injuries, but I could only laugh at them.

I liked being a winner and I figured I would have to tolerate a bit of pain to be one in my game. As far as I was concerned, there was no such thing as "the pain barrier". Some people can tolerate pain, some people can't. Pain is basically the "hurting", and if someone wants to achieve something he'll put up with more of the hurting. There have been plenty of times when I have been in pain on the football field, and when play slowed or the injury first happened, I would often feel the pain fiercely. But when I put my mind back onto what was happening in a match, I seemed to forget about the pain. I put my body through hell each Sunday for 80 minutes, and in that I was no different to most players.

I've been accused of play-acting on the field and taking swan dives. I'll admit there have been odd occasions when I have gone down to slow up the game and give my team-mates time to regroup, but why would I take dives? The referees were never going to penalise the other team because of me, that was for sure! In my last couple of seasons I got a lot of knocks to the head, and was taken out behind the play or hit with high tackles, but I rarely got a penalty. I would have had to been shot or stabbed for that.

Those illegal knocks I received were the main reasons I was often left wobbly kneed, clinging to a trainer. People thought I was either play-acting or a miracle man to be able to go back into the play as if nothing had happened. Neither was correct and to be honest I couldn't care what people thought. I have never given myself the warrior image; the media whacked that on me. And I

The Sometimes Philosopher

never tried to live up to it. The simple fact was that I hated coming off before the end of a game and I hated missing games. I did all I could in both cases to avoid that happening.

I loved the game and wanted to put as much into it as I could. That still applies, but when it comes to what some see as the logical progression from playing to coaching, I doubt that it will happen to me. I know how much time and effort a player has to put into the game, and a coach has to put in more. A coach's family must suffer twice as much. He has to watch match videos, set skills training, work out tactics, be a father confessor, as well as deal with the media each day. I don't think I would be equipped for it, and I don't think administration is for me either. I'd get into too much bother. Coaches have been blamed for making the game too programed, but I disagree with claims that Sydney Rugby League has lost its flamboyancy or excitement and that it is based too much on defence. The game now is 70 per cent faster and harder than when I entered Rugby League in 1976. The much-improved defence game has made players faster, fitter and smarter and improved the level of tactics needed to break those defences.

There may not be any teams like Canterbury of old who could throw the ball through 16 pairs of hands 10 times a game, but there are some great tries being scored these days and players definitely have better skills and think more about the play than 10 years ago. The bottom line these days is that if you are not fit and can't think, there is no room for you in first-grade Rugby League—and I'm talking about the fullback right through to the front-rower.

Administrators have to keep up with the times as well, but a lot hasn't changed in that department over the years. John Quayle has replaced Kevin Humphreys, the League has become incorporated, and a couple of businessmen attend their board meetings, but generally the same people are running things. John Quayle is a good man, an honest man, but he is a member of the board which also employs him, and that is a ridiculous situation. I wonder if he is little more than a figurehead at the NSW Rugby league?

Ken (Arko) Arthurson has been a heavyweight figure in the game since he was a very successful secretary at Manly. I've always regarded him as a terrific bloke and he has always seemed to have more power than anyone else, but that seems to be one of his problems. He is always trying to be a nice bloke and does too many people too many favours.

When it came to the Australian Rugby League, good old Ron

McAuliffe has run the game as much as anyone else. Arko may have been the chairman, but wily old McAuliffe, the Queensland League supremo and ARL deputy-chairman, seems to have dictated a lot of what was decided at national level.

Ultimately, the administration can make or break the game, much like the media being able to make or break a player. I found it very hard to get on with the media in my first few seasons, but eventually I realised how powerful media people and coverage could be in anyone's football career.

Often a press bloke would call me up and have a long conversation about things, take out one quote, distort it and make headlines. I learned from experience how to watch out for this. When I became captain I naturally had a lot more to do with the media and I became more relaxed and mellow.

I often thought some press guys couldn't think for themselves. If they were in the pressbox and one of the them said, "Gee Billy Bloggs is having a whale of a game", all the papers the next day would say Billy Bloggs had been sensational. Another thing I objected to, at times, was the overdramatisation of isolated brawls or punch-ups. If a great game had featured five fantastic tries, chances were the brawl in the 10th minute would make the headlines, not the football. Generally the media have been very good to me, however, and I think today most players and media people, with a few exceptions, understand each other and have a good working relationship.

Having been on one side of the fence, and now finding myself on the other has made my entrance into the media and the first year of my radio career a whole lot easier. It is something which I really see as a challenge, and I have attacked it with the same enthusiasm I did my playing days. I have a lot of improving to do, and a lot of that will be in my vocabulary, but I'm working on it.

John White started negotiating a radio career for me towards the end of my last season. It's good that 15 years of hard slog as a player can land me something like that. I had agreed to join 2UE shortly after I finished playing, but then I pulled out. I thought I had retired to be with my family, and now I was going to be away weekends working on radio. I had wanted to watch Ben play soccer every Saturday and share more of his childhood with him. Radio 2UE was great. Executives there talked it over with me and offered to do whatever they could so that the job wouldn't interfere. It's even in my contract that Ben's soccer has priority and there's a helicopter available whenever I need it to make a quick dash to the football on Saturdays. The shows starts at noon but I don't come on until 1pm, mostly so I can watch Ben play soccer first. Often Ben comes to the football with me and sits in the box or 2UE organises a seat for him outside.

I've known my co-commentator Ray Hadley since we were kids. He also played for Dundas Rugby Union, one age group behind me, but he was never much of a footballer. Even then he wanted to be a race caller. At club barbecues Hadley would have everyone organised in a phantom race call, but he didn't have much variety in his act—the horse which came down the outside always won.

Another person who used to go to those Dundas Valley barbecues, and whom I also crossed paths with professionally many years later, was John White. He ended up being like an older brother to me, and I would never have achieved what I have in football if it hadn't been for someone like him.

Rugby League is nearing total professionalism and despite club secretaries and some players being suspicious of them, well-intentioned player-managers are priceless. If there were a few more John Whites going around, a lot more players would be happier.

I was a footballer and a carpenter. I was no negotiator. The more of my energies I could put into playing the game, while letting somebody else take care of off-field matters when it came to negotiating my contract and other worries, the better it was for me. Player-managers will become the norm in a few years, but I don't like those who are in for a quick buck or who don't have the player's welfare at heart. I advise players to tread warily when they look for someone to manage their affairs.

I had no worries on that score with Whitey. In fact, he has never charged me fees, or to be more precise, wouldn't accept fees, during our 10-year association. He took it upon himself, as an old family friend, to look after my welfare and has helped me in every facet of life. The only way I could repay him was to try to live up to his expectations on the field and with an occasional gift instead of money.

John has known my family for 30 years. He used to live in the street parallel to ours at Dundas and coached my brother Donald for a while in Rugby Union. He can be very strong-willed and pig-headed like me, but he has always had Ray Price at heart.

While League is getting more professional, I don't think it will

Two sides of the media: Ben waits as I am interviewed by Channel 10's Graeme Hughes after a match; and after retirement and in radio with 2UE commentator Ray Hadley, an old Dundas Rugby Union acquaintance.

ever become a full-time profession for players. There are some players now who regard themselves as "professional footballers" but that's just another way of saying they don't want to work. My good mate Peter Sterling fell into that category. On the field he was the true professional, but off it he was hopeless. He went through jobs like I went through bootlaces and he has been quite content not to work in the past few years. He would spend most of his time either at the races, down the TAB, on the tennis court or in bed asleep. But don't think that attitude was reflected in his football. When it came to playing and training, he gave nothing less than 100 per cent.

Good luck to him, and the other so-called professionals, I suppose. They obviously enjoy their midweek games of golf and tennis, and the repeats of the repeats of *Days Of Our Lives*. But it was never for me.

I have always maintained it was good for a player to have a full-time job outside his football, and for only 12 months of my career did I not work. Being a carpenter, I was always an early starter, and in the late 1970s I set up my own firm. For quite a few years I'd leave early in the morning before the kids were up and three nights a week I went straight to training and got home after they were in bed. For that reason, I had 12 months as a professional footballer.

Then Whitey got me a job as a sales rep at his firm, Davco Services, which deals in ceramic tiles and adhesives. I had a go at it for a couple of years, but I was no white-collar worker and, despite Whitey always being at me, I couldn't come to grips with wearing a tie. So I didn't.

In the last couple of years I've gone back to being self-employed in a partnership with Whitey's brother Eddie (everyone calls him the Whale). We don't work flat out because the taxman would get too much of our money, but we are kept pretty busy.

I've always been a 7am starter, including Mondays. When I played Rugby Union it was no effort at all to get up early for work on Mondays because we played Saturdays and had Sunday to get over it. In my first few seasons in League, when we played mostly on Sunday, I used to drag myself out of bed with my body aching all over, but as I've said, working the day after the game was the best way to sort out my aches and pains.

The building game suits me. I have always liked to get out in the open air with a T-shirt on, or go shirtless in summer. I've never been attracted to a life in an office or on the road, and my type of job was good for my fitness, discipline and eye for detail, which are all important parts of Rugby League.

Jack Gibson used to tell us a player's personality on the field reflected his character off the field. I was a worker.

A Look Back

WHEN I LOOK BACK on 16 seasons of first-grade Rugby Union and Rugby League, I realise it has not been as easy a path as many people may have imagined. I am no different to most footballers. Professional sport brought me great benefits along with the sacrifices, financial rewards but plenty of hardships, and my life was virtually taken over by something within which told me to keep pushing, keep achieving, keep tolerating. Rugby League can be like a drug. The addiciten can take over your life.

The most important thing about sport has always been the enjoyment it brought me. It was the one thing in my life I could excel at, and at the same time I simply liked doing it. There were other sides to Rugby League, outside the 80 minutes on the field, which have occasionally made the going tough, though rarely have I wondered whether it was all worth it.

My wife Chris would probably say no, then she would think about it further and say yes. I would have no hesitation in saying yes; it was all worth it, despite the loss of my privacy, and the strain that that, plus the time involved in being a player, put on my family.

The rewards have been plenty. There have been some great moments of elation and satisfaction that could never be replaced: the chance to set up my family at a more comfortable level of living that would not have been possible if not for Rugby League; the opportunity I was given to become a respected figure of society that someone from my background could usually only dream about; and most of all, League has brought me lasting friendships, and they are the richest things in life.

What my career meant to me was put into perspective a few days after the day I retired, on 1986 grand-final day. It all became

Winners together: Neville Wran, the longest serving Premier of NSW, with me and my Dally M Award in 1982.

A Look Back

clearer on the Wednesday night at a celebrity roast to cap off Mick Cronin's and my testimonial year.

There were more than a thousand people crammed into the Parramatta Leagues Club auditorium that night. They were seated on the terraces above the lifts and in every far corner of the room. They weren't rich people. I'm sure many were real strugglers. But they had dug into their pockets and come along just to say thanks to Michael Cronin and Ray Price for giving them some enjoyment over the years.

I'll never forget the strange feeling of sitting there next to the Crow on the stage, isolated from everyone else, with the lights shining in our eyes and stopping us from identifying anyone in the sea of faces. And sitting right in front of the Crow was a whole jug of Bacardi and coke.

Jack Gibson and Ron Massey got up and took the micky out of us. Then Peter Sterling repeated the trick. Comedian Ray Seager, a Parramatta fan and one of the funniest men I know, had started the ball rolling earlier. Ray Warren and Ray Hadley compered the whole thing and had their cheap shots as well. But then Terry Fearnley, my first coach at Parramatta and a man I'll always admire and respect, capped it off. He got a rousing cheer from the audience who were so glad to see him back at Parramatta, but he told them he didn't want to "roast" us. He preferred to be sincere. What he said went down very, very well.

It was probably the next day when it all sunk in. All the eulogies had been said: 16 years of first-grade football (in Rugby Union and Rugby League) had come to an end. I came home from work that day and for the first time in a long, long time I went to my study and pulled out two suitcases of souvenirs my family had collected during my playing days. There were scrapbooks that Chris and my mum had kept, a stack of photos I had collected, telegrams from all sorts of people, and videos of special games. I was up all night, reminiscing, and the memories that kept flashing-back to me were almost as clear as if the events had occurred yesterday.

I laughed when I saw how rough I had looked when I played Union for Parramatta, with a scraggy beard that was so thin it looked like bumfluff, and my hair halfway down my back, always kept off my face by black electrician's tape. I pondered some quotes from my Union coach Rod Phelps, who was a kind of "Jack Gibson" before his time. I went through some clippings from my only Wallaby Tour in 1975–76 and remembered that I was so frustrated by injuries on that trip I nearly stayed in Union another year to prove something that could have changed my entire life.

Going back to the beginning of my League days, I thought of blokes like John Peard, and the 12 tries I scored in my first season, 1976, most of which were from his high kicks. Peardy was one of the big reasons why Parramatta that year started a whole new era of success.

Crucial to that success were guys like Graham Olling. Two years before I went to Parramatta Shovels was an 80 kg (12½ stone) weakling playing park football with Wentworthville. He realised that he wanted to be a Sydney first-grader, and was so determined he went on steroids. He worked every day on his body, always pumping iron and running up the steps of City Tattersalls Club with a lead scuba diver's belt around his waist. Through sheer guts and determination he went on to play for Australia as a prop and became one of the most feared players of his time.

There was John Baker; and always the mystery around how old he was. He was playing first grade in about 1969 and was still at Parramatta in 1981. He must have been at least 35 then. Baker was the hardest player pound for pound I ever played with or against. Ray Higgs was from the same mould. It didn't matter how big the opposition were, both Higgsy and Baker knew how to hurt them.

Ron Hilditch was among them. How do you describe old Tanglefeet? He was an awkward athlete and one of the tallest hookers ever to play the game, but he won a trip away with the 1978 Kangaroos and showed he could also play prop. He became one of the biggest hitters in League.

Then came Jack Gibson. He was unique. He moulded a team of incredibly talented youngsters around "old" blokes like Steve Edge, Mick Cronin and myself. At first there were some geriatrics like Bob O'Reilly and Kevin Stevens. Gibbo was thought mad to keep that pair on the "pension", but who was laughing when we were doing Parramatta's first ever victory lap in 1981?

When I had emptied out the suitcases I looked around the trophy cabinet. Winning the Caltex-NSW Sports Star of the Year in 1979 was one of my proudest achievements, because it had judged me along with people from all sports. I had a heap of Dally M trophies, the big one plus five for lock of the year. In 1980 I had spent a fair time out injured and since then I have missed lock of the year only once when I was injured and that was when Steve

One of the truly special moments: being chaired off by Steve Mortimer and Garry Jack after my last Test match for Australia in 1984, the Third Test against Great Britain which we won 20–7.

Rogers got it in 1981. He won the gold Dally M and Mick Cronin got the award for the centre position. So Sludge who had played about six games at lock, got "my" award, even though I got the International of the Year award. I won the gold Dally M the next year and in 1983 I could have become the only player to win it twice, but I was sent off for "tripping" with two weeks of the competition remaining and me ahead in the points count. That referee's decision, which I will debate till the day I die, cost me the award and a few thousand dollars. I vowed then that I would win the Dally M lock award until I retired. It was another goal I achieved in my final year.

I picked out a colour picture of me holding up the 1986 National Panasonic Cup. That meant so much as well. Both Mick Cronin and I had been out (I was injured, Crow was suspended, if you can believe it) the only other time Parramatta had won it in 1980. It was the first competition the Eels had ever won and I was so dirty that I couldn't play in the final I promised I'd get my revenge before my playing days finished. It proved to be another fairytale.

There were my medals sitting together: the Harry Sunderland Award for the best player from the 1978 Test series against the Poms; the Rothmans Medal from 1979. (Crow had won it the previous two years and Ray Higgs the year before that.)

Sticking out most of all was my Order of Australia medal. I was the first Rugby League player to receive the award, in 1984. Clive Churchill and Mick Cronin each received one the following year, which made me realise even more the career parallels my good mate Mick and I had enjoyed.

Being honoured by your country is the ultimate accolade. It showed that sport was able to lift people who might not have enjoyed wealthy backgrounds, a good education or simply a rails run in life. Orders of Australia and MBE's and Knighthoods usually go to artists and authors and politicians. Only a few of us have received such honours for just enjoying ourselves on the sports field.

I went to bed pretty late that night, my head full of great memories, thinking that this boy from Dundas had done all right. I had been just one of a heap of kids who had grown up the tough way in an area looked down upon by many people. As I put my head on the pillow I was sure I was the luckiest of them all.